Have you ever tried to choose a book to give your child . . . and not known what to select?

A toy or a shirt can be judged at a glance . . . but books take more consideration. It's often true: you really can't tell a book by its cover.

So you either select something blindly . . . or return to an old favorite from *your* childhood . . . or give up and buy a toy instead.

Kathryn and John Lindskoog's book is an answer to this dilemma. These two parents—a teacher and an author—have faced the same problem . . . and have done thorough research and reading to solve it.

HOW TO GROW A YOUNG READER is a browser's guide to children's literature, beginning with the first book for children in 1671 and ending at the present. Each chapter presents new treasures for your child— the classics, tales of fantasy, realistic fiction and biography, Christian novels, poetry and nonsense, fact books, recorded readings—and how to devise some recorded and written classics of your own. . . .

Here's the key to over 400 books that will provide enjoyable reading for you and your children!

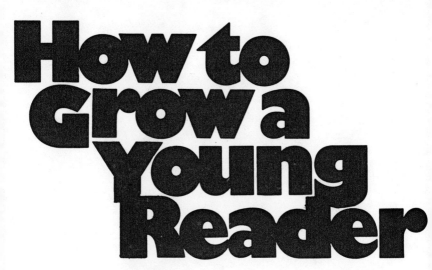

How to Grow a Young Reader

John & Kay Lindskoog

David C. Cook Publishing Co.

ELGIN, ILLINOIS—WESTON, ONTARIO

Acknowledgment
Our thanks to the Orange Public Library for making much of our research possible.

HOW TO GROW A YOUNG READER
Copyright © 1978 David C. Cook Publishing Co.

Published by David C. Cook Publishing Co., Elgin, IL 60120
Edited by Janet Hoover Thoma
Designed by Kurt Dietsch
Cover photo by Jim Whitmer

Printed in the United States of America
Library of Congress Catalog Number 78-54994
ISBN 0-89191-115-4

First printing—July 1978
Second printing—November 1978

To Jonathan and Peter
Our guides through parenthood.

Contents

Preface

My most delightful early childhood memories are of bedtime stories—especially fairy tales.

Then, when I was six years old, I made a most amazing discovery. One idle afternoon I suddenly realized that the mysterious rituals we had been practicing in first grade made it possible for me to read stories to myself. I didn't even have to say the words aloud; I could hear them more quickly through my eyes! I had a magic power of my own as wonderful as any in the fairy tales. I didn't have to wait for bedtime anymore.

Since then, good books have been both the bedtime and morning stories of my mental life—some giving me repose and others awakening me. Books bring me closer to people and God. Books have informed me when I was ignorant and consoled me when I was suffering. They have guided me to joy and meaning and have actually healed me when I was sick. They have set off explosions of ideas in my mind. They keep me laughing and caring and growing.

Good books have made my life good. Through books I learn the wonder of the ordinary. And I walk next to all kinds of people, sharing their thoughts and experiences.

But no book can be really complete in this life; it has to end where the author's time and understanding end. There is always something left unsaid. I look forward to the life to come as the unending last chapter of all the good books I have ever read.

The Golden Age Is Now

The Riches of Children's Literature Today

It has always seemed clear to me that a good book for children must be a good book in its own right.

John Rowe Townsend
A Sense of Story

ONCE UPON A TIME the wisest man who ever lived warned grimly, "There is no end to the writing of books. . . ."[1]

True, but little could King Solomon dream of the endless supply of books today.

Solomon lived about one thousand years before Christ, in what was the short golden age of the kingdom of Israel. With all his ambition, power, and intelligence—not to mention his one thousand wives and untold number of children—he probably never

11

imagined the possibility of even one book for children. And with all his silks and ivory and spices and gold—over twenty-five tons a year—he would surely have been amazed by the wealth of talent and beauty invested in children's books today. They are a new kind of treasure.

Solomon was rather a failure as a parent, according to the Old Testament. And although he was the richest and wisest king, he was even somewhat a failure at that. But he was a great writer, if you believe that he wrote all the parts of the Bible attributed to him.

One piece of advice he gave was "Never ask, 'Oh, why were things so much better in the old days?' It's not an intelligent question."[2]

Solomon is implying that things were not really better then, and in children's literature, this is true. Today, not yesterday, is the prime time.

In 1950 it seemed wonderful that over fourteen hundred new children's books were being published in the United States yearly. This was twenty times as many as any child would read in a year, if one believes the supposition that children between seven and fourteen read an absolute maximum of seventy books a year.

But today there are almost three thousand new children's books published yearly, double the number in 1950. Because many books continue to be printed year after year—if not decade after decade—almost forty thousand children's books are now in print in our country.

And American children also benefit from books published in Great Britian, where approximately three thousand new books for children are also being published yearly. Although some are duplicates of new books in America, most are not.

It is said that the twenty years between 1950 and 1970

gave British children the richest harvest of imaginative books any nation has ever produced. An extraordinary revival of folktales, fairy stories, fantasies, and myths is occurring on both sides of the Atlantic.

Of course, only part of these thousands upon thousands of children's books are top quality. Children's books are profitable for hack writers and publishers who don't mind imitating others or reissuing old books in inferior editions. After all, books are simply merchandise to many people in the publishing business.

But if only a quarter of these books are really excellent, that still means ten thousand top quality books are available in the United States alone—with over seven hundred added each year.

The few periodicals that describe new children's books to teachers and librarians can't begin to keep up with them all. Subscriptions to these journals have soared since 1950. And now thousands of short reviews from various periodicals are being collected into reference volumes.

Some people may want to cry, "Stop the presses! Enough is enough!" But if the gigantic children's publishing business should collapse, we would lose the new favorites that burst upon us every year.

And so we not only have lists of good books, we now have lists of the lists of good books! (You can get such a list free by writing for "Choosing a Child's Book" from Children's Book Council, 67 Irving Place, New York, NY 10003, and enclosing a large, stamped self-addressed envelope.)

One basic list parents could consult is a list of the prizewinners. Ironically, the two top American awards—the Newbery and Caldecott Medals—are named after Englishmen.

13

John Newbery, who died over two centuries ago, was the first major English publisher of books for children. Every year since 1922, the American Library Association has chosen the most distinguished children's book by a United States author from the previous year. There are usually several honor books named as well.

The same committee of twenty-three librarians awards the Caldecott Medal for the best picture book by an American artist. This prize, which began in 1937, is named in honor of Randolph Caldecott, an English illustrator of a century ago whose pictures still delight some children. Both the Newbery and Caldecott awards were originated by Frederic G. Melcher, who was editor of the influential American periodical *Publisher's Weekly*.

A third major award is a $1,000 prize, contributed by the Children's Book Council at the National Book Awards annual convention. It was first awarded in 1969, after twenty years of National Book Awards limited to adult books.

Ironically, the key award for good children's books in England is named after an American—Andrew Carnegie, the millionaire who contributed generously to libraries in both countries. Similar to the Newbery Medal, the Carnegie Medal is awarded to the author of a book published in the previous year. Since 1969 the author does not have to be a British subject, but the book must be in English and have been printed first in the United Kingdom.

England's counterpart to our Caldecott Medal is the Kate Greenaway Medal, in memory of one of England's favorite illustrators. These English medals are also awarded by panels of librarians.

There is one outstanding international award, the Hans Christian Andersen Award, established in 1956 by the International Board on Books for Young People. It is awarded every two years to a living author who has made an important international contribution by his complete work, rather than a single book. Five different countries are represented on the selection committee, and, since 1966, they also award a medal to illustrators.

However, as Solomon said, "in this world fast runners do not always win the races, and the brave do not always win the battles."[3] Likewise, the really best books do not always win the prizes. *The Lion, the Witch and the Wardrobe* by C. S. Lewis didn't win any prize. It entered the world quietly in 1950—but for many people, it split our century in half.

"This is no thaw," a dwarf said to the winter witch in Lewis's story. "This is *spring*." And, for children's books, 1950 really was.

[1]*Good News Bible,* Eccles. 12:12.
[2]Ibid., Eccles. 7:10.
[3]Ibid., Eccles. 9:11.

2

Reign of the One-eyed Dragon

TV in Our Time

Television captures the imagination but does not free it. A good book at once stimulates and frees the mind.

Bruno Bettelheim
"Parents vs. Television"
Redbook, November 1963

IRONICALLY, 1950, which was the turning point for modern children's literature, is the very year that marked the takeover of family life by television. For between 1948 and 1952, television entered about fifteen million American homes. One cannot honestly think much about children's literature without considering television, because many people believe it has usurped reading time and probably undermined reading ability. What is the place of television in the American home today? And what are some of its possible effects?

No one can measure the differences between television families and television-free families now, because there aren't enough television-free families to provide a random sampling. Only one home out of one hundred lacks television, and the other ninety-nine approach two sets per home.

In one survey, 82 percent of all parents believed that television was good for their children: they felt it was relaxing or educational. Preschool children spend more than a third of their waking hours watching TV—instead of talking and playing—and some researchers extend this to over half their waking time. A preposterous fifty-four hours a week is the figure usually quoted.

That means a child spends more time watching TV before kindergarten than he will spend in four years of college classes. Ten-year-olds may spend more hours per week watching television than attending school. And an ordinary twenty-year-old I read about figures that she has already spent 20,000 hours of her life watching television. That is conservative.

Author and scientist Isaac Asimov has brushed aside the menace of widespread TV addiction by claiming that people who watch a lot of television would be doing other things equally as empty—like staring into space. He assumes that they would be passive even without their television sets, accomplishing nothing.

That's a radical assumption to make about the average adult who watches TV twenty-one to thirty-five hours a week. Thirty hours of nothing? Perhaps that is how average adults look to a man like Asimov. But, in fact, people who have to do without television for a time generally resort to reading, hobbies, games, studies, longer family dinners, earlier bedtimes, and even improved sex lives, according to some reports.

HOW TO GROW A YOUNG READER

Asimov seems to be considering children as basically inactive, because children watch television more than any other group. But when they are not watching television, children are about the busiest people in the world. They are constantly exploring themselves and their environment, chattering, reflecting, insisting, and probably keeping at least one adult very busy. Their brains, the most complicated things on earth, are developing daily. Most of their healthy growth activity falls into one category—play. Play is child's work.

And reading is child's work. When we read, our minds decode and manipulate the lines we see, in a tremendously complex symbolic transformation. The cost to the reader is great concentration, and one of his benefits is enriched powers of imagination. The reading mind visualizes. The reading mind sets its own pace and even stops or goes back for better comprehension or deeper response. The reading mind is extremely active.

Needless to say, humans are not apt to invest great concentration in this mental activity called reading if they have become dependent upon a fascinating machine, which discourages analysis, imagination, and integration. Aside from floating in the womb, there are few states of mind more passive than TV watching.

As Marie Winn points out in her extraordinary book *The Plug-in Drug: Television, Children, and the Family,* the first television generation would have been about three years old in 1950, when television boomed. So we could expect to see the possible results in young people who approached college age in 1964 or 1965. Did that generation really show any new tendencies that could be a result of television?

It just happens that in 1964 the reading and writing ability of high-school students who took college board exams suddenly dropped. And just as childhood television watching has steadily increased since 1950, so students' verbal abilities have steadily declined. This certainly does not prove that spending five to ten thousand hours watching TV before first grade interferes with the proper development of verbal ability, not to mention other abilities and attitudes and relationships. But the coincidence is suspicious.

Some people assume that hours of adult words and phrases pouring from a mechanical box should improve children's vocabulary and self-expression. But since it obviously hasn't, Marie Winn suggests that prolonged television viewing permanently retards the development of the brain's left side, where the center for logical speech is located. No matter what the program content, looking at moving images produced on a screen by tiny dots is going to have some physiological effect upon the eyes and brain.

She even suggests that video overstimulation of the brain's right half may cause the increased tendency toward drug abuse, which became obvious in the 1960s. Such a theory is far-fetched, but so are most theories that prove true in the long run.

So far the effect of six hours of flittering images a day on an immature, developing brain has never been scientifically studied. It would be too callous and cruel an experiment for scientists to inflict upon an innocent child, although kindly parents do it to their children all the time. So theories, statistics, and suspicions are almost all we have to go on.

Of course, some people go on intuition, assumptions, or what they call common sense. E. B. White, author of one of this century's best books, *Charlotte's Web,* isn't waiting for any future analysis of children's brain development. He simply declared in *Newsweek,* "Short of throwing away all the television sets, I really don't know what we can do about writing." That was in 1975 in an article discussing "Why Johnny Can't Write."[1]

No wonder Johnny can't write, since he has to be a good reader to be a good writer. And today we also have the problem of why Johnny's parents can't read— parents who grew up in the 1950s. Five adults out of a hundred in our country can't read. And vast numbers fall into a new category called "lazy readers." They don't seem to visualize or concentrate well.

In fairy-tale terms, children today seem to have inherited an incredible treasure of books but are held spellbound by a cold magic eye. Some children are born with reading disabilities. Others seem to derive them from a kindly electronic dragon who keeps them close company at home. He was brought in as a pet to pacify and entertain them.... but wise old stories warn us not to trust dragons.

3

Battle Strategy

Family Reading Possibilities

The child who is exposed naturally, as part of a happy home life,
to the best work of good writers, is fortunate indeed.

Frank Eyre

British Children's Literature in the Twentieth Century

CHILDREN GAIN inner growth from rich reading, but they often need practical encouragement at home.

Obviously, the main deterrent to good reading in the home is television. Families who try to control overactive television sets have found a variety of strategies that help, as well as many that fail. Different families need different solutions to such a problem.

The modest improvement that one family made was to cut their children's viewing down to three hours a day. For them, that was success. Many other families have tried—successfully or unsuccessfully—to set one hour a day as maximum TV time. Needless to say, in some homes the one hour expands and expands because of wheedling, needling, whining, pleading, bargaining, and sneaking. Parents get worn down.

Also, it is just about impossible for parents to limit television when they are not home, because most baby-sitters use TV to amuse themselves and the children. Many baby-sitters simply aren't used to TV rules and purposely ignore them. Television has become the baby-sitter's baby-sitter.

A few unusual families make television a weekend indulgence only. And even then it may be limited to a few hours. All of this requires strong enforcement. So does television "rental," where family members buy TV time by doing chores or paying money into a book fund or by reading books first.

In contrast to parents who allow sets in their children's bedrooms, some parents limit the family to one set and keep it in an inconvenient place, such as the basement or garage, where viewing is less comfortable. Others store a small set in a closet and find that children are less apt to watch it if they have to get it out and then put it away afterwards.

Another gambit that might work for a few parents is to watch television with the child, making value comments whenever needed. This sharing is good for the child and an eye-opener for the parent. When the parent can't or won't watch any longer, the set goes off.

A natural method of limiting television use is to neglect to repair or replace an aging set. Poor reception discourages viewers who are not severely addicted. And the ultimate extension of that course of inaction is to neglect to replace a set when it expires.

Alas, turning off the television doesn't automatically turn on books. The telephone, the doorbell, and all the clamor of demands and delights and discomforts are still there. Certain people will, it is said, keep reading even if the house is on fire. But in typical homes today the trick is to foster reading when the house isn't on fire. In some homes that is a difficult trick, which requires some mundane planning.

The first way to prepare children for literature is to talk a lot to them and to take pleasure in human sounds with them from the beginning. Nancy Larrick, in *A Parent's Guide to Reading*, suggests four weeks as the right age to start preparing a child to become a reader. When words and love have always gone together in a child's life, he may grow up loving words themselves.

The basic way to interest children in good books is to have good books in the home. Ideally, children should see both parents reading, and even hear their parents talk about books. Unless you have some good reason for not doing so, buy some of these books. It has been said that the United States won't ever be a very literate nation until we spend as much for books as we do for chewing gum.

How many parents spend as much time reading as watching television? How many go to the library as often as the drug store? Or to the bookstore as often as the shoe store? Not many if we believe these statistics: the average American doesn't read one book a year, and over half the people in the United States haven't read a book in the last five years.

Children notice where parents go and how they spend their money. Taking children along to libraries and friendly bookstores can be fun for everyone.

C. S. Lewis said his father bought all the books he read

and never got rid of any of them. His description of their turn-of-the-century Irish house in his autobiography, *Surprised by Joy,* is famous.

> There were books in the study, books in the drawing room, books in the cloakroom, books (two deep) in the great book-case on the landing, books in a bedroom, books piled as high as my shoulder in the cistern attic, books of all kinds reflect-ing every transient stage of my parents' interest, books readable and unreadable, books suitable for a child and books most emphatically not. Nothing was forbidden me. In the seemingly endless rainy afternoons I took volume after volume from the shelves. I had always the same certainty of finding a book that was new to me as a man who walks into a field has of finding a new blade of grass.

That is one extreme. We see the other extreme all too often.

Even if they own just a few books, many families keep them stashed away at the back of a closet. Bookworms seek them out anywhere, but for normal children, books should be visible in the home. Besides deserving a special shelf or bookcase, they can be purposely propped in public places to tempt people.

One family built a book display rack for current interests beside their dining table. Another family has a full bookcase in their large bathroom. One bachelor interior decorator says that he leaves unusual books open in his glamorous New York apartment to make his rooms look "read in." Of course, his purpose is style rather than substance. But that proves that bookish houses need not be dowdy. A parent who cares can set out different books from week to week for variety, the way some people set out vases of flowers or dishes of candy.

In many homes a space may have to be set aside so a

child who does not read easily can have a quiet and well-lighted place. In a busy and crowded house, where there is more than one child to a bedroom, a young reader could be given the privilege of reading alone in his parents' room. Some children like to read curled up in giant beanbags, which plop on the floor anywhere.

Daylight is the best kind of light for the eyes, when it is available. Many fluorescent light bulbs emit rays that are tiring and irritating to sensitive people and can cause hyperactivity or emotional strain. Parents should be cautious about using these lights where their children read. Simply watching for undue fatigue, restlessness, and crankiness will tell most parents if their children suffer from this common sensitivity, which could secretly spoil a reading area.

And there are quite a few children who become too restless to read well after eating sweets. The average American now eats an incredible 94.7 pounds of sugar a year! Perhaps that creates mental as well as dental cavities in some children.

Restlessness often interferes with listening as well as reading. A relaxed pace and a pleasant—(not preachy or sugary)—tone of voice are always helpful. The better the oral reader, the better the attention. Needless to say, even calm young children like to participate when they are listening. A skillful reader can involve the child with short questions and answers and invitations to join in on refrains.

But sometimes reading aloud successfully is absolutely impossible. Some children can't ever listen until they are settled in bed for the night. And some hyperactive children listen best while they are soaking and swishing in the bathtub. Water is magically calming to them and enables them to enjoy a story better.

Countless other story times have been destroyed by outside interruptions. At meals or at bedtime it is often worthwhile to take the telephone off the hook and hang a note by the doorbell in order to have privacy.

Reading aloud should be comfortable for parents if possible. Perching on the side of a bunk bed or a water bed is dreadful. Lying down beside a child puts some tired parents to sleep. Some can keep on "reading" a few sentences of utter nonsense as they drift off—much to the listener's consternation.

One father bought a sturdy old recliner chair for seven dollars at a garage sale for the sole purpose of reading to his son at bedtime. He realized that he had gradually given this up because they had physically outgrown their lap-sitting and bed-sharing days, and an upright chair or the floor was discouraging. The large comfortable chair helped.

Reading patterns should and do vary immensely from family to family. Some homes encourage reading at meals, and others consider it a vice. Some let babies tear up old magazines and let toddlers scribble in their picture books if they want to; others consider that a sacrilege. Some families can read in cars on trips, and others think it is bad for the eyes and/or nauseating. One book that would be fun to read aloud in the car is E. B. White's *Stuart Little,* a story about a mouse's auto journey.

For families who find story reading impossible in moving vehicles, group memorization of limericks and other favorite poems makes an enriching diversion from time to time.

Books taken on vacations or visits can redeem spare moments. They give children pleasure in unfamiliar bedrooms and campsites. They can also enrich long waits on all kinds of ordinary errands.

How long should parents continue to read aloud to their children? Long after the children can read well to themselves. Children enjoy hearing stories that are far beyond their reading level. They need that stretching. The parent has the double pleasure of sharing old favorites and making new discoveries with a maturing child. For many children, there are few times more cozy and secure than when parents are reading to them. The physical closeness and the sound of that attentive voice continue to nurture us, even in our memories. And what parent doesn't cherish this same sharing?

In today's hectic, high-pressure society—full of confused and neglected children and frustrated adults—the battle for family reading is one small part of the war that love is waging.

4

The Story of Children's Literature

Dear, dear! How queer everything is today! And yesterday things went on just as usual. I wonder if I've been changed in the night?

Lewis Carroll
Alice's Adventures in Wonderland

ONCE A CHILD wants to read, the spotlight is on books—where it should be. In order to appreciate children's literature, let us return to the past, where for thousands of years, things went on as usual: there were no books for children.

The printing press was invented in 1437, but early books were for adults. The first English printer, William Caxton, brought out a set of old animal stories called *Aesop's Fables* for adults, and it became very popular with children and is still read today.

28

The hornbook was invented about 1500 for children's education, but it wasn't really a book. It was a sort of wooden paddle for school lessons—the alphabet, numerals, and the Lord's Prayer. Sometimes these paddles were also used on the playground for hitting balls, supposedly leading to the British game of cricket.

Chapbooks came into existence at about the same time, but *chapbook* was simply a way of saying "cheap-book." These books were as flimsy as hornbooks were sturdy, and they had nothing to do with education. They were little pamphlets usually sixteen pages long, illustrated with crude woodcuts and costing about one penny. Printed mainly for the poor—who made up 85 percent of the population—they consisted of condensed versions of well-known tales like Robin Hood and King Arthur, legends, and fairy tales.

Much like primitive comic books, they were peddled by chapmen who carried them in bundles. Illiterate people were fascinated by the pictures and would gather to hear the stories read by someone who could read. Unfortunately, there wasn't much reading in these books that remained popular with children and adults in England and America for two centuries.

In the midst of this literary poverty, the first English translation of the Bible, by Miles Coverdale, was published in 1537. In 1611 the King James, or Authorized, version was published.

Puritan children on both continents were limited to the Bible and a few acceptable books, which they could only open with properly washed hands and a high regard for decorum. Books were brought out on Sundays, opened in silence, and often followed by little oral examinations. If fortunate, the children were allowed to read an adult favorite, Foxe's *Book of Martyrs*, which was popular in the

1600s although it was a century old by then. This exciting book railed against the pope and was illustrated with copper engravings of dead and dying Protestants who gave their lives for God—highly entertaining violence with a Christian message.

The first real literature for children in England and America consisted of gloomy Puritan tales of sin, death, and hell, designed to steer children into eternal life. For example, in 1671 James Janeway wrote *A Token for Children: Being an Exact Account of the Conversion, Holy and Exemplary Lives, and Joyful Deaths of Several Young Children.* He urged children to live godly lives before dying joyfully with Christ's name on their lips. Godly living consisted of not doing a lot of things, such as playing with toys—especially Satan's favorite, the spinning top.

Children who failed to live right would go to hell. But those who succeeded would be rewarded by an early and joyful death and everlasting bliss. Janeway himself died at 38—how joyfully is not recorded.

In the same year a typical "courtesy book" for teenagers of the day was written by Caleb Trenchfield, Gent., and titled *A Cap of Gray Hair for a Green Head: or, The Father's Counsel to His Son, an Apprentice in London.* Like Charles Shedd's *Letters to Philip,* this book gave advice to a young man concerning proper behavior after marriage.

Trenchfield cautioned, "Women can with no patience endure to be mew'd up till Mid-night while you are clubbing it at a Tavern; and you cannot think it a wonder, if at such times they sport with your Servants at home. . . . How long is Love to last, where the blundering Husband comes home like a sous'd Hogshead . . ."

The greatest Puritan book beside Milton's masterpieces was John Bunyan's *Pilgrim's Progress,* written for adults but relished by children. Published in 1678, it sold at least a hundred thousand copies in Bunyan's lifetime and will be discussed more fully in chapter eleven.

Shortly after *Pilgrim's Progress,* American Puritans produced the *New England Primer* to teach children to read. Its rhyming alphabet begins:

A . . . In Adam's fall
We sinned all.

B . . . This life to mend
God's book attend.

Editions of the primer varied, and there were other sections, such as "Spiritual Milk for Boston Babes" and a long message from a Christian martyr, John Rogers, accompanied by a picture of him burning up while his wife and ten children watched—held back by a guard. The primer, which was subtitled "An Easy and Pleasant Guide to the Art of Reading," sold six-to-eight million copies and was used for over a century.

In contrast, across the Atlantic in 1715 Isaac Watts published *Divine Songs* for children. Watts was a Puritan clergyman and hymn writer whose lyrics contained an unusual softness and beauty. His many songs included the well-known "Cradle Hymn" (Hush! my dear, lie still and slumber), "When I Survey the Wondrous Cross," "Joy to the World," and "O God, Our Help in Ages Past."

Soon after the lovely Watts hymns, two adult books were published that soon became children's favorites since children still had no stories of their own. These were Daniel Defoe's *Robinson Crusoe* (1719), which is strongly Christian in its full-length version, and Jonathan Swift's *Gulliver's Travels* (1726).

Then a certain trickle entered England that would later become a flood. In 1729 a popular French book was

31

translated into English: Charles Perrault's collection of eight fairy tales entitled *Tales of Mother Goose*. Children loved it. It was a far cry from their old Puritan books—although morals were tacked onto the tales, such as this one at the end of "Little Red Riding Hood."

Little girls, this seems to say,
Never stop upon your way.
Never trust a stranger-friend;
No one knows how it will end.
As you're pretty, so be wise;
Wolves may lurk in every guise.
Handsome they may be, and kind,
Gay, or charming—never mind!
Now, as then, 'tis simple truth—
Sweetest tongue has sharpest tooth!

After thousands of years of reading and writing, this was the earliest piece of literature for children that intended to entertain more than instruct. It came only 250 years ago!

Next came the first man to successfully produce books for children: John Newbery. His motto was "Trade and Plumb-cake for ever. Huzza!" That meant "Business and entertainment—hurrah!"

A farmer's son who married a printer's widow in Reading, England, he took over her first husband's business and moved to London. Soon he became a publisher, a bookstore owner, and an author. It is now known that he hired two great London authors as ghost writers to help him turn out the books he printed: Oliver Goldsmith and Dr. Samuel Johnson.

A growing number of people had the time, money, and education to buy books and read. Middle class families were becoming more home and family centered.

And children were being recognized as special human beings. Newbery was the first to realize what a market there was for books produced especially for children. Starting in 1744, he published over thirty children's books.

A shrewd businessman, Newbery died rich. But most of his wealth was gained from the sale of patent medicines rather than books. His best known remedy, Dr. James's Fever Powder, is mentioned often in his children's books. In fact, a tragic death occurred in one story because the sick person was unable to obtain this marvelous medicine.

The Newbery family handed the formula down through several generations until it was destroyed in the London blitz during World War II. The powder was probably based on antimony and was highly regarded for two centuries as a remedy for humans and cattle.

The first Newbery book announced on its title page: "*A Little Pretty Pocket Book*, Intended for the Instruction and Amusement of Little Master Tommy and Pretty Miss Polly with Two Letters from Jack the Giant Killer, As Also A Ball and a Pincushion, the use of which will infallibly make Tommy a good Boy and Polly a good Girl . . ."

Amusement is the key word. Newbery wanted to amuse while teaching. The book cost sixpence, and the ball or pincushion two pence extra. Pins were to be stuck into the ball's one side or other to record the child's good and bad deeds. The book contained a series of games with rhymed directions, such as pitch and hussel, cricket, and leap frog; it also included proverbs, rules of behavior, a rhyming alphabet, and a few poems.

Newbery invented characters and imaginary authors including Woglog the Giant, Giles Gingerbread (a boy

33

who lived on learning), Nurse Truelove, Peregrine Puzzlebrains, and Primrose Prettyface.

His best publication was *Goody Two-Shoes,* described on the title page as "The History of Little Goody Two-Shoes, otherwise called Mrs. Margery Two-Shoes, with the means by which she acquired her Learning and Wisdom . . . See the original Manuscript in the *Vatican* at *Rome,* and the Cuts by Michael Angelo. . . ."

Of course, the original manuscript of this story was not at the Vatican. But Newbery liked little jokes, like his pretense about Michelangelo.

In 1751 Newbery brought out the first children's periodical of all time, *The Lilliputian Magazine,* which pretended to be produced by the Lilliputian Society and its secretary R. Goodwill. Four years later he published the first children's Bible, *The New Testament Adapted to the Capacities of Children.* The Puritans hadn't done that!

At about the time of the American Revolution, Isaiah Thomas of Massachusetts pirated Newbery's books and made them available to American children apparently without paying Newbery a penny.

At the turn of the century, Christian tract societies were established in England and America to minister to adults and children. Sunday School Unions were being formed then also. In 1820, the Tract Society of New York (later the American Tract Society) warned that books of fiction and fancy were a bad influence and that books of war, piracy, and murder led children into crime.

In 1825, the Philadelphia Sunday School Union published *The Glass of Whiskey* for children. It said, "There is a bottle. It has something in it which is called whiskey. Little reader, I hope you will never take any as long as you live. It is a poison. So is brandy, so is rum, so is gin, and many other drinks. They are called strong drink.

34

They are so strong that they knock people down and kill them."

In the early 1800s educated people as well as religious persons disapproved of imaginative literature for children. They preferred factual information about science, history, geography, or travel to fairy tales or other improbable or absurd books.

Samuel Griswold Goodrich agreed with them, and in 1827 he published *Tales of Peter Parley About America*. It was so popular that he wrote 120 other information books under the pen name Peter Parley. Sales reached 7,000,000, and there were numerous imitations in both America and England.

At about the same time, the Grimm brothers' collection of German folk tales was translated into English, a foretaste of the gain creative children's literature would soon make. The Grimms were German language scholars who took a professional interest in traditional fairy tales and wrote out dozens and dozens in faithful detail.

In 1837, Victoria took the throne of England; and before her reign was over, the tide turned, and children's literature exploded with creative fiction and fantasy.

Two years after she was crowned, the earliest fairy story was written by Mary Sinclair in her book *Holiday House*—"The Wonderful Story."

Fairy stories, in contrast to fairy tales, are original stories of marvelous happenings created by modern authors that echo the old tales. Mary Sinclair's story is about a lazy, greedy boy named Master No-book, and it begins, "In the days of yore, children were not all such clever, good, sensible people as they are now." As you can tell, the story is cheerful satire.

Two years later a twelve-year-old girl named Euphemia Gray challenged the young adult John Ruskin to write a fairy story for her. She thought it would be impossible, but Ruskin promptly wrote *The King of the Golden River*. When it was published ten years later, he and Euphemia were already married.

"The Wonderful Story," *The King of the Golden River*, and several other fine stories from the 1800s are now in the collection *Modern Fairy Stories*, edited by Roger Lancelyn Green.

In 1844 Francis Paget published *The Hope of the Katzekopfs: or, The Sorrows of Selfishness*, thinking that a tale of enchantment might teach wisdom to young people. Paget was rebelling against "the unbelief of this dull, plodding, unimaginative, money-getting, money-loving nineteenth century."

Two years later, Hans Christian Andersen's *Fairy Tales* was translated into English. The incomparable Andersen had collected and retold folk tales from various lands and added fairy stories of his own.

Four years after Andersen's stories came to England, the public library movement began there in 1850. That seems like a dull fact, but this movement would eventually make good books available to vastly more children and would be a great support to children's book publishers.

In 1851 Ruskin's *King of the Golden River* was published, and for fifty years after that children's literature continued to flourish.

Series books also became extremely popular at this time. There were adventure series, mystery series, biography series, and series on sports, science, and occupations. In the books of the American Horatio Alger, a poor boy always makes good through hard work: the epitome of America itself. Beginning with *Ragged Dick* in 1868, Alger wrote over a hundred books, mostly in series of six. He was not a significant writer, but he was surely a significant phenomenon. Though few read his books today, his name is a household word.

Another category of literature that came into its own in the Victorian age was the domestic drama. The first great example is *Little Women* (1868) by Louisa May Alcott. Then there was Martha Finlay's series of *Elsie Dinsmore* (1867), books about the most goody-goody heroine in all fiction. In addition to being very rich and beautiful, this little girl is extremely tearful. She cries sixty-three times in the first book alone.

In his book *Written for Children,* author John Rowe Townsend says, "The fascinating thing about Elsie is that although she is so pure, and the tone of the books is religious and uplifting, the reader nevertheless can wallow in emotion and sensuality while contemplating those beautiful large soft eyes, forever filling with tears; that slender frame forever being clasped to Father's breast for kisses and fondlings. This perhaps is the literary equivalent of 'tonic wine,' which you can drink without guilt but which is quite highly alcoholic."

In 1881 *The Five Little Peppers and How They Grew* by Margaret Sidney appeared, telling about a resourceful family and the mother who works hard tailoring and mending to pay their rent. The first book led to a series of six and sold over a million copies.

Frances Hodgson Burnett's *Little Lord Fauntleroy* (1885) went through nine editions in nine months and is said to have swept England like a sickly fever. Burnett's *The Secret Garden,* which came out twenty-five years later, is considered a much better book.

One of the most powerful and imaginative Victorian fantasy writers was George MacDonald, a Congregational minister turned author, who had an enormous influence on C. S. Lewis years later. His works for children include *The Golden Key* (1867), *At the Back of the North Wind* (1871), *The Princess and the Goblin* (1872), *The Princess and Gurdie* (1883), *The Light Princess* (1893), and several short stories. Here is a Christian author who wrote serious yet exciting fairy stories.

With a few notable exceptions, children's literature became far less exciting in the first half of the twentieth century. Then something happened around 1950, and another flood of outstanding books appeared. The children's book wealth of the atomic age rivals that of the Victorian age or exceeds it. The books of the twentieth century will be discussed in later chapters. Aside from quality, the numbers alone are staggering. Juvenile literature has become big business.

In 1940 Random House, one of the largest publishers in the United States, had no separate juvenile department. But by 1973 their juvenile budget alone was $13,000,000, and that department was their most profitable. They have entire warehouses covering several acres to store the books of just one of their most popular authors—Dr. Seuss.

Dr. Seuss began as the mere Theodor Geisel, a Hollywood screen artist and successful advertising cartoonist. He wrote his first book by accident, setting words to the rhythm of the ship's engines on a long crossing of the Atlantic. His first two books under the pen name Dr. Seuss were so popular that he became a full-time children's author.

He has no children of his own, and it has been said that he is not particularly fond of children. It is also said that he has sold more books than any other living author and is probably the richest writer alive. If so, he must be one of the very richest in the history of the world.

Three hundred years ago little American children were reading:

Xerxes did die
And so must I

in their New England Primers. Today they are reading:

We looked!
Then we saw him step in on the mat!
We looked!
And we saw him!
The Cat in the Hat!

Dr. Seuss wrote *The Cat in the Hat* with only 223 carefully chosen words, a controlled vocabulary for beginners. Now he no longer believes in the controlled vocabulary. But he still thinks that we wouldn't have so many illiterates today if they had been given interesting reading materials as children.

An incredible amount has happened between Perrault's *Mother Goose* and Dr. Seuss. Our children who sample the literature in between are richer for it.

5

Old Books for Young People

If one man's meat is another man's poison, certainly one man's book may be another man's boredom.

May Hill Arbuthnot
Children's Books Too Good to Miss

HERE IS A BROWSER'S GUIDE to thirty of the best books from the past for children today. They are not better than today's books just because they are older. But they are part of our heritage and too good to forget.

Early copies of these beloved books are extremely valuable, but current editions of the same books are cheap and plentiful. Dover Publications sells facsimiles of children's classics from eighteenth century chapbooks on. All are high quality at low prices.[1]

The writers of this literature were not all innocent,

domesticated, pious, and happy, although one was Queen Victoria's chaplain. One was a political spy, one took his pen name from his job as a rowdy riverboat pilot, and one had to endure her husband's mistress living in her household. One was the unhappy, successful secretary of the Bank of England; one grew up hungry, his father in debtor's prison; and one killed her mother in a fit of insanity. Two were famous linguists, and one, who fought both tuberculosis and strict religion from boyhood, became an engineer, a lawyer, and a popular author—only to die young. Those who wrote some of the greatest children's books of all time were as varied as the books they produced.

ROBINSON CRUSOE by Daniel Defoe (1719)

A major character in a great detective novel says, "When my spirits are bad—*Robinson Crusoe*. When I want advice—*Robinson Crusoe*. In past times, when my wife plagued me: in present times, when I have had a drop too much—*Robinson Crusoe*. I have worn out six stout *Robinson Crusoe's* with hard work in my service."

Written for adult readers, *Robinson Crusoe* is one of the most popular adventure stories ever told. It has given rise to many imitations, the most famous being J. D. Wyss's *Swiss Family Robinson*.

The main part of the story, which is supposedly based on the real adventures of Alexander Selkirk, begins when Robinson Crusoe is shipwrecked on a solitary island near the Orinoco River. Adjusting to the primitive conditions by practicing self-reliance and ingenuity, he builds a shelter, raises corn, makes a raft, and finds great comfort reading the Bible. After twenty-four years of solitude, he finds a companion, the Negro Friday, whom he saves from cannibals on that day. Later on, ship-wrecked survivors join him, and he eventually returns to England.

Defoe was the son of a Presbyterian butcher in London and was in the butchers' trade himself for a time. But he was a born journalist. Once he began writing, he wrote countless political pamphlets and single-handedly produced a journal called *The Review* three times a week for ten years.

One of his political pamphlets was a satire urging the high-church Anglicans to be more severe in their persecution of Protestants. When the Anglicans realized that he was really attacking them for their intolerance, Queen Anne had him severely fined, pilloried, and cast into Newgate prison for two years.

Defoe's political sympathies were fickle, swinging between the Whigs and the Tories. He even spied for each side, sometimes simultaneously, while he ran a hosiery business. Sophisticated writers of the day, such as Jonathan Swift, who wrote *Gulliver's Travels*, considered Defoe illiterate.

Defoe was almost sixty when he wrote this first novel and discovered his gift for vivid fiction. After that he wrote two sequels and a series of other novels in his last ten years, obviously turning them out as fast as possible for fun and profit. Of varying quality, they are landmarks in English literature.

GULLIVER'S TRAVELS by Jonathan Swift (1726)

This book appeals to adults because of its satire on human institutions and to children because of its fantasy. In its first three weeks it sold 10,000 copies.

Jonathan Swift was dean of the Cathedral of Dublin,

Ireland, but spent a great deal of time in London and was active in political life. He was passionately devoted to the welfare of the oppressed and wrote this book to attack all manner of evils, lampooning the English in particular. Because it is a masterpiece, they loved it anyway.

The book has four parts:

- Lemuel Gulliver, a ship's surgeon, sails from Bristol, is shipwrecked, and swims ashore to find himself on the island of Lilliput, whose inhabitants are foolish and petty and only six inches tall.

- Gulliver next finds himself in Brobdingnog where he treats those citizens as the Lilliputians treated him. This portion is a satire on politics.

- The islands of Laputa and Lagado are the scene for less memorable adventures that satirize the endeavors of philosophers and scientists.

- Finally Gulliver visits the land of the Houyhnhnms, where a race of intelligent and kind horses rule over a race of stupid and filthy humans known as Yahoos. After trying to describe our civilization to the Houyhnhnms, Gulliver realizes that all humans are Yahoos.

In its entirety, this book is too negative for many adults and certainly too harsh for children. But there are good expurgated versions that both children and adults can enjoy.

TALES FROM SHAKESPEARE by Mary and Charles Lamb (1807)

Here twenty plays by Shakespeare are turned into stories for young readers. They are retold simply and with faithfulness to the originals, emphasizing the moral of the central situation in each play. Shakespeare's own language has been woven into the text wherever possible. Mary wrote the fourteen comedies; Charles the six tragedies.

Charles and Mary were a devoted brother and sister who inherited brilliance and the family tendency toward insanity. Charles lost his mind and was committed once, and he never knew if the illness would reoccur.

Once, after his recovery, he returned home and found Mary holding a bloody knife: she had just injured their father and killed their mother.

Charles became Mary's legal guardian and cared for her from then on, thus sparing her life in an asylum but forfeiting marriage for himself. When she was not suffering occasional relapses, Mary was a loving and delightful companion. But Charles had to support them both by working in an ordinary job, writing his popular essays and his part of this book in his spare time.

FAIRY TALES by Jacob and Wilhelm Grimm (translated into English in 1823)

These noted German linguists became intensely interested in the relationship of language to folktales. For thirteen years, they went from village to village and house to house transcribing folk and fairy tales.

The first English edition of their work, called *German Popular Stories,* contained fifty-five tales in two volumes. It was illustrated by George Cruikshank, whose vigorous but eerie etchings enhanced the stories. (Years later Cruikshank became a crusader against alcohol and rewrote some of the stories as propaganda for abstinence.)

With this publication the crude, oral folktales enjoyed by the uneducated and illiterate suddenly became literature, heralding a new era. Others would begin to explore legend and lore around the world, and their work would inspire the creation of new tales of wonder and fantasy.

The Grimms's stories are not really full of fairies. There are tales of kings and princes, ordinary folk such as tailors and soldiers, and apprentices in search of their fortune. Magic abounds; goblins weave spells; and birds, beasts, and people avenge bad deeds or aid the good-natured. Some stories are pure beast fables. Others are familiar stories in a new guise, such as "The Sleeping Beauty" and "Cinderella."

One of the best poets of our century, W. H. Auden, claimed that the Grimm tales should not only be given to children, but are "an educational 'must' for adults." In his opinion, "it is hardly too much to say that these tales rank next to the Bible in importance." They are not, of course, Christian.

A CHRISTMAS CAROL by Charles Dickens (1843)

This story of nineteenth century England has delighted young and old for over a century. Novelist Dickens wrote his *Christmas Books* for family reading in five years, and *A Christmas Carol* became the most popular. His little *Life of Our Lord,* which he wrote for his own children in 1849 and not for publication, was finally printed in 1934 but is not widely known.

A Christmas Carol tells about miser Ebenezer Scrooge who dreams he is visited by spirits on Christmas Eve that enable him to see his past life—his miserliness and his danger of eternal hell. On Christmas Day, he awakens a changed man. The carol ends with the joyful cry of Tiny Tim, the crippled son of Scrooge's needy clerk, Bob Cratchet, "God bless us, every one!"

Dickens is best known for such novels as *Oliver Twist*

(1838), *David Copperfield* (1850), *A Tale of Two Cities* (1859), and *Great Expectations* (1861).

FAIRY TALES by Hans Christian Andersen (translated into English in 1846)

Danish Hans Andersen, the gangling and awkward son of a poor washerwoman and a shoemaker, was often ridiculed and mistreated by his peers. His profound love of children and compassion for their suffering is evident in his *Fairy Tales,* which are considered to be among the most beautiful, sensitive, and powerful tales ever told. Fancy and reality blend in these stories, which include "The Little Match Girl," "The Ugly Duckling," "The Little Mermaid," and his masterpiece, "The Snow Queen."

WATER BABIES by Charles Kingsley (1863)

Charles Kingsley was a scholar in mathematics and classics at Cambridge University and after ordination became the parish priest at Eversley. He immediately set out to reform the parish. He was co-founder of the Christian Socialist movement in Britain and a professor at Cambridge. In 1859 he became chaplain to Queen Victoria.

He wrote *Water Babies* for his youngest child, Grenville. The hero is a neglected little chimney sweep named Tom who drowns in a river and becomes a water baby, to be helped by good fairies. Tom swims to the home of other water babies, where he meets the two fairies Bedonebyasyoudid and Doasyouwouldbedoneby who slowly teach him to be good. The theme of this strange moral fantasy is redemption: Tom is washed from sin.

ALICE'S ADVENTURES IN WONDERLAND by Lewis Carroll (1865)

The Rev. C. L. Dodgson (Lewis Carroll) taught mathematics at Oxford University. He was a bachelor who was interested in logic, photography, and little children—so long as they were girls, not boys.

During a boat ride with a colleague's three daughters on July 4, 1862, he began telling the girls a story. Later he wrote it down at the request of his favorite, Alice, calling it *Alice's Adventures Underground.* This handwritten illustrated manuscript is in the British Museum.

Once Carroll decided to publish the book, he chose the famous *Punch* illustrator John Tenniel to do the pictures. By then Alice was becoming a teenager, who according to Carroll had "changed a good deal, and hardly for the better," and was too mature to be Tenniel's model. So the real elfin, brunette Alice was replaced by the blond girl we all know so well.

The publication was a story in itself. Dodgson commissioned Macmillan and Company to publish the book, paying for it himself. In his own words, he inflicted on the company "about as much wear and worry as ever publishers had lived through."

When the final proofs were approved, it was printed by Oxford University Press, and 2,000 copies of the pages were delivered to Carroll. He immediately sent them to Macmillan, asking that fifty copies be bound as soon as possible for gifts, plus one special copy in white vellum for Alice.

When they were completed, he began to worry about the quality of printing and the illustrations and decided to have the entire work reprinted. Most friends and relatives who had been given the 1865 copies dutifully returned them and later received 1866 copies, which were actually in the bookstores by Christmas, 1865.

What happened to the rest of the original 2,000 copies, which had cost Carroll 350 pounds? They were sent to the United States to be sold, and Carroll received 120 pounds for them. Apparently he did not mind if the inferior edition appeared that far from home.

In spite of some poor reviews, the book was immediately successful, and by the 1880s had been introduced in most European countries including Russia, where the title became *Sonya in the Kingdom of Wonder*.

Alice has been of immense interest to adults, but many children today are bored or disturbed by it. Most of the wit is lost to modern children and much of it to adults, unless they read an annotated version that explains the jokes and puns. It and its companion book, *Through the Looking Glass,* which was published in 1871, are the source of numerous familiar quotations.

Critics have a field day analyzing this book for psychological symbols. Many contemporary critics assume that there is something inherently sinister about a bachelor professor who was a devout Christian and took superb photographs of little girls as a hobby.

Alice Liddell (*the* Alice) died in 1934, but lived long enough to celebrate the Lewis Carroll centenary in 1932 and to autograph a copy of the book for the present Queen Elizabeth.

HANS BRINKER, OR THE SILVER SKATES by Mary Mapes Dodge (1865)

This story was published at the end of the American Civil War by the first editor of the famous old children's magazine *St. Nicholas.* Contributors to the magazine included Louisa May Alcott, Henry Wadsworth Longfellow, Rudyard Kipling, Emily Dickinson, and John Greenleaf Whittier.

Under Dodge's thirty-two-year editorship, *St. Nicholas* became the world's best children's magazine and influenced children's literature for many years. It circulated across the United States and to foreign nations, and letters from grateful children poured in by the thousands. Today people can enjoy thumbing through one of the delightful anthologies that are usually available in public libraries.

Hans Brinker is the story of a young boy's efforts in a distance skating competition in nineteenth century Holland. The mystery and suspense is interwoven with educational information about the history and customs of Holland.

LITTLE WOMEN by Louisa May Alcott (1868-1869)

Here is the first great family story, based on the author's own life. Alcott's editor talked her into writing a girl's story, instead of the fairy stories she had been trying with no success. Both Alcott and her editor thought the finished work might seem dull. But it was a best seller and was followed by *Little Women, Part II* and others.

The little women are the four very human daughters of the memorable March family in New England: Jo, Beth, Meg, and Amy. This nineteenth-century family struggles with various problems, including the prolonged absence of the father and the death of loved ones. Jo, the strong young heroine, becomes a writer like Alcott and goes on to lead a full and active life.

Alcott also wrote *An Old Fashioned Girl* (1870) and *Little Men* (1871).

AT THE BACK OF THE NORTH WIND by George MacDonald (1871)

In this extremely powerful story, reminiscent of Andersen's *Snow Queen,* Little Diamond, a coachman's son, has two parallel lives—one in the harsh world of working-class London and the other in a dream world where he travels with the North Wind, who is a beautiful woman. He is carried through thirty-eight adventures (chapters), some with the North Wind and some with earthly friends or enemies—a continual change back and forth between the fantastic and the realistic.

Little Diamond reforms, rescues, and guides several people; he gets sick and passes through the North Wind to the country lying at her back. Because of its sad beauty, this book is probably for very few children; but it is superb for adults.

Two of MacDonald's other books, *The Princess and the Goblin* (1872) and *The Princess and Curdie* (1883), are highly appealing to children. Furthermore, twenty of MacDonald's other stories are now available in a two-volume set called *The Gifts of the Child Christ: Fairy Tales and Stories for the Childlike.* The two favorites in that set are "The Golden Key" and "The Light Princess."

Although MacDonald was a minister plagued with poverty and tuberculosis, he did eventually become a celebrated literary figure. He was so spectacular on a lecture tour in the United States that he was offered the pastorate of a church on New York's Fifth Avenue with a salary of $20,000 a year. He was also invited to coauthor a novel with Mark Twain. MacDonald's literary talent can't compare with Twain's, but his power of imagination makes him Twain's equal.

C. S. Lewis was strongly influenced by MacDonald's

writing. As a Christian he said that he owed more to MacDonald than any other single person. In *The Great Divorce,* a short fantasy for adults, Lewis pictured himself meeting George MacDonald on the outskirts of heaven and telling the wise old man how his writing led him to Christianity.

BLACK BEAUTY by Anna Sewell (1877)

A semi-invalid, Anna Sewell wrote this book in her last years "to induce kindness, sympathy and an understanding treatment of horses." Published the year before her death, it was the first animal story of major importance.

The horse, Black Beauty, tells this story, which abounds with accounts of cruelty to animals—certainly not exaggerated. But some adults chuckle, because the horse-narrator all too often expresses the tastes and opinions of a refined lady of the 1800s. Nevertheless, Sewell wrote with compassion and courage, condemning both war and fox-hunting when that was a highly unpopular stand to take.

An imitator wrote a dog story, *Beautiful Joe,* in which a dog looked at the pictures in his mistress's copy of *Black Beauty.* At the end Beautiful Joe says, "Now I must really close my story. Good-bye to the boys and girls who may read it; and if it is not wrong for a dog to say it I should like to add, 'God bless you all.' " Compared to *Beautiful Joe, Black Beauty* is fine literature.

THE PETERKIN PAPERS by Lucretia Hale (1880)

One day Lucretia Hale and some friends were about to go for a drive, but their horse refused to budge. After trying every method possible, they discovered they had forgotten to untie it from the hitching post. This event is supposed to have provided the idea for her Peterkin stories. The Peterkin family manages to complicate all sorts of simple situations.

These problems are always solved by a certain practical lady from Philadelphia. Obviously, the humor is robust and simple.

UNCLE REMUS by Joel Chandler Harris (1880)

Joel Chandler Harris collected about seven hundred tales that he heard slaves tell in his native state of Georgia. He attributed them all to the excellent memory of his fictitious slave Uncle Remus. The tales center around Brer Rabbit who repeatedly triumphs over other animals. Like several other children's books, *Uncle Remus* has been criticized as being insensitive towards blacks.

The Margaret Wise Brown version of this book, called *Brer Rabbit,* is the simplest one to read.

TREASURE ISLAND by Robert Louis Stevenson (1883)

On a cold, windy, and wet Scottish vacation with his parents and his stepson Lloyd, R. L. Stevenson drew a map of an imaginary island and began writing a story about it to entertain his stepson.

If you want a Christian book, you won't find it here. But you will find raw, mutinous, hard-core adventure. All the rules for writing children's stories were broken. Blood appears; morality disappears; and the rum flows freely. But, of course, the young hero survives.

Stevenson himself was a Scottish lighthouse-builder's son who disappointed his doting parents—in his schooling, his choice of friends, and his religion. He married a divorced Californian, cruised the Pacific twice, and settled on the island of Samoa.

HEIDI by Johanna Spyri (English translation, 1884)

This story about a happy, joyful girl who loves life in all its fullness and overcomes misfortune is set in Switzerland. Following the wholesome tradition of *Hans Brinker, or the Silver Skates,* it portrays the land and people well.

THE ADVENTURES OF HUCKLEBERRY FINN by Mark Twain (1884)

The journey of Huck Finn, son of a drunken scoundrel, and his friend, the runaway slave Jim, down the Mississippi River is one of America's greatest works of literature. The symbolism of the river has perhaps been overworked by some critics, but there is great life and energy as well as sheer laziness in this story of suffering, joy, and escape. America was itself in a time of great adventure, and this story mirrors that.

Samuel Clemens worked as a young riverboat pilot on the Mississippi and derived his pen name, Mark Twain, from a call that sounded the depth of the water.

The Adventures of Tom Sawyer, though not generally regarded as highly by experts, is an excellent story that many children enjoy even more. Twain was one of the great humorists of all time, but under the humor one finds an increasingly sad, serious, and even bitter man.

THE HAPPY PRINCE AND OTHER FAIRY TALES by Oscar Wilde (1888)

The tales told by Oscar Wilde are highly polished and

full of imagery. The most famous is "The Selfish Giant," which audaciously brings Jesus into a fairy tale that combines gentle humor with overwhelming sweetness.

Oscar Fingall O'Flahertie Wills Wilde led a life as flamboyant as his name. He claimed that he poured his genius into his life and only put his talent into his writing. Although he was hailed as a master of adult wit and drama, he died a broken man only twelve years after he published his fairy tales. It seems as if we are fortunate to inherit the fruits of his talent rather than the fruits of his genius.

THE BLUE FAIRY BOOK by Andrew Lang (1889)

Although Mrs. Lang and others did the retelling, Andrew Lang did edit a series of fairy books known as the "Colour Fairy Books." The first one was *The Blue Fairy Book*, featuring tales from Grimm and Perrault, old chapbook stories, some selections from *The Arabian Nights*, some Scottish tales, and an abridged version of *Gulliver's Travels*. His subsequent color books, which ended in 1910 with *The Lilac Fairy Book*, branched out and included fairy lore from all over the world.

PINOCCHIO by Carlo Lorenzini (first English translation, 1891)

Written by an Italian who used the pen name Collodi, this story has been popular in the United States ever since it was translated into English. A carved wooden puppet comes to life and is repeatedly saved from the results of his foolishness and sin by the Blue Fairy. Children enjoy the wickedness of Pinocchio and his eventual transformation from a bad puppet to a good boy.

THE JUNGLE BOOKS by Rudyard Kipling (1894-1895)

These two volumes are much more interesting than most animal stories, because Kipling's writing is unusually inventive and colorful.

The story of the boy Mowgli, raised by wolves and destined to become leader of the jungle, is well-known. Although these stories are said to teach children about nature—highlighting the similarities and differences between humans and animals—they certainly do not give the most accurate portrayal of animal life. Instead, they express Kipling's own code of masculine behavior.

Kipling also wrote a series of fanciful animal tales for younger children, the *Just So Stories,* which are good to read aloud. However, there is some keen objection to the self-concept of the black boy in "How the Leopard Got His Spots."

THE STORY OF THE TREASURE SEEKERS by Edith Nesbit (1899)

Edith Nesbit knew both wealth and poverty. When she was young, her widowed mother lost all her money, and later her husband lost his business capital because of a dishonest partner. She had to support the family herself, which she did in a variety of ways, including the hand-coloring of Christmas cards and, eventually, by writing books for children. At one time her husband even brought a mistress home to live with his wife.

The Treasure Seekers was her first book and the beginning of a series about the Bastable children, who appear digging for treasure, selling poems, serving as detectives, rescuing a princess, and borrowing money. The principal character is Oswald Bastable, the oldest boy and also the narrator. Although he does not say that he is the narrator, it is obvious because he refers to Oswald as "a boy of firm and unswerving character" and makes other self-congratulatory remarks.

The other two Bastable stories are *The Wouldbegoods* and *New Treasure Seekers*. Nesbit wrote a second set of three books about a family of children who fall into fantastic adventures: *Five Children and It* (1902), *The Phoenix and the Carpet* (1904), and *The Story of the Amulet* (1906). C. S. Lewis mentioned the Bastables at the beginning of his own children's book *The Magician's Nephew*. He was particularly fond of *The Story of the Amulet*.

THE WIZARD OF OZ by L. Frank Baum (1900)

Here is a highly moral fantasy of midwestern America that is often underrated. Many libraries have refused to carry it, thinking it junk literature. Ironically, the English saw its value.

L. Frank Baum was a kind of rollicking wizard himself. While he was still in his teens, he became a journalist and established his own weekly newspaper while he sold fiction and humorous verse to magazines. He wandered the Middle West as a traveling salesman, became a successful producer of several dramas, wrote for various large newspapers, and founded the National Association of Window Trimmers!

With a wife and four sons to support, he also worked as a hack writer for a fiction factory, turning out twenty-four girls' books as Edyth Van Dyne and more books as Susanne Metcalf, Laura Bancroft, Floyd Akers, Capt. Hugh Fitzgerald, and other unlikely people.

In 1899 Baum's own book *Father Goose, His Book*, which

told stories about nursery rhyme characters, sold 90,000 copies in ninety days. With the profits, Baum built a summer home on Lake Michigan called "The Sign of the Goose," made his own furniture, decorated the house with geese details, and crowned the project with an immense stained-glass window featuring a goose. (Then he wrote a book about decorating.)

The next year *The Wizard of Oz* came out and was quickly made into a New York musical. Baum got the name Oz from the O-Z drawer on a filing cabinet. The story of Dorothy's adventures with the Scarecrow, the Tinman, and the Cowardly Lion has always been popular with children and has even spawned an Oz cult among adults.

In 1905 Baum moved to Southern California, eventually settled in Hollywood in a home called Ozcot, and became the dahlia-growing king of California. After several successive Oz books such as *The Land of Oz* and *Ozma of Oz*, he tried to end the series with *The Emerald City of Oz*, but pressure from children kept the series going until there were fourteen. After Baum's death, even more were produced by inferior writers.

THE TALE OF PETER RABBIT by Beatrix Potter (1901)

Beatrix Potter (1866-1943) was the best writer and artist of picture-story books at the turn of the century.

She grew up a lonely, shy child of very wealthy and neglectful parents; her editor/fiance died shortly before their wedding; and in her later years she married a rich English farmer and became quite a crusty and unsentimental land owner. She never had any children.

Her classic *Tale of Peter Rabbit* and other stories created a little world of amusement and delight. Young children fall in love with Hunca Munca, Squirrel Nutkin, Mrs. Tiggy-Winkle, Jemima Puddle-Duck, and the others. Her watercolor illustrations, which show cozy little animals dressed up like humans, pursuing their busy lives in meadows and lanes and doll houses, and the clear, precise art of the text make her work a milestone in children's literature. It is claimed that *Peter Rabbit* is the beginning of the modern picture-story: a total blend of picture and text.

In a satirical essay, the contemporary author Rumer Godden creates an imaginary correspondence between a tasteless modern editor and the ghost of Beatrix Potter, in which she is urged to simplify her vocabulary and change the story for modern children. She replies, "I have too much common sense to think that *Peter Rabbit* could ever be magnificent; he is an ordinary small brown rabbit."

In a letter to *The Horn Book* in May, 1929, the real Beatrix Potter wrote, "My usual way of writing is to scribble, and cut out, and write again and again. The shorter and plainer the better. And read the Bible (unrevised version and Old Testament) if I feel my style wants chastening."

REBECCA OF SUNNYBROOK FARM by Kate Douglas Wiggin (1903)

In an era when both American nostalgia and concern for female self-esteem are flourishing, this sweet, light-hearted, and witty novel deserves a reading. It is the story of a gay young girl who has to be brought up in a small town by her two rigid, gloomy, and suspicious aunts. Guess who brings up whom!

Anne of Green Gables by L. M. Montgomery (1908) is a similar but definitely original story about another spunky girl.

Both of these books are well written and present positive, well-balanced images of vigorous girlhood.

PETER PAN by James M. Barrie (1904; 1911)

Peter Pan was first the hero of a play (1904). The author later made the play into a book, *Peter and Wendy* (1904). The book has never been as popular as the play, because its language is a bit subtle for children. A musical version of the play, starring Mary Martin, was produced around the middle of the century.

The story features Peter Pan, the boy who will not grow up, Captain Hook, the fairy Tinker Bell, and the three Darling children, who go off to Never Never Land with Peter. Darling really is a family name, but *Wendy* was never heard of until Barrie invented it for his young heroine. Few writers have invented a new name that has been bestowed upon so many children.

WHITE FANG by Jack London (1906)

This is a story of fierce animal heroism. White Fang is a crossbreed dog who is cruelly trained to be a ferocious fighter. Later a kind owner domesticates him, and he eventually gives his life to save this man.

Jack London lived a short, rough, and extremely adventurous life that began in poverty and ended in suicide. His writing enjoyed great popularity in his day. Another dog story of his, *The Call of the Wild* (1903), is probably his greatest single success; it, too, is enjoyed by many children.

THE WONDERFUL ADVENTURES OF NILS by Selma Lagerlof (translated into English 1907)

The National Teachers' Association of Sweden asked Selma Lagerlof to write a geographical reader about Sweden. She spent three years studying the folklore and natural history of the provinces and wrote this work of genius. *The Wonderful Adventures of Nils* came out in 1906, and *The Further Adventures of Nils* in 1907. Now they are combined in one volume.

Lagerlof presents Sweden's climate, landscape, wild creatures, people, and traditions through the experiences of young Nils, a farmer's son. Nils is bad-tempered and unkind to animals. He becomes an elf who rides on the back of a wild goose and is soon enlightened. One favorite episode is the great crane dance on a mountain near the sea.

In 1909 Lagerlof received the Nobel Prize in Literature, the first woman to ever receive that honor.

THE WIND IN THE WILLOWS by Kenneth Grahame (1908)

Here is a book that evokes nostalgia, one that can be read to young children or savored by older readers.

The author was a country gentleman who loved the outdoors. His father abandoned him and three other children to their grandmother after their mother died. Instead of getting the education he was suited for, Grahame went into banking and became wealthy before he retired to the country.

Grahame enjoyed telling long tales to his son "Mouse" at bedtime. Once when Mouse was to go to the seaside with his nurse, he put up a terrible fuss because he would miss the story's continuation. His father persuaded him with the promise that he would mail him a chapter a day. The nurse returned these chapters to the Grahames, sensing their value. They became *The Wind in the Willows*.

Each chapter contains an adventure of four animal friends—Mole, Water Rat, Badger, and Toad. Morality, though never mentioned, permeates all the action and conversation of the animals—really "people in fur" that represent human types.

The animals live a lovely pastoral life along the river. But not far from there is the Wild Wood and beyond that the Wide World, where river animals would never go if they had any sense. Toad doesn't, and gets himself into all kinds of trouble. He is rescued in the end by his friends, and the idyllic life is once again resumed.

THE SECRET GARDEN by Frances Hodgson Burnett (1909)

This is the wonderful story of an unhappy and physically handicapped boy named Colin and the two children who worked a change in him. All three children eventually blossom through their creative contact with the mystery of growing things in the mysterious secret garden.

The thirty books described in this chapter are all from before World War I. The children who first enjoyed them are now grandparents, great-grandparents, or have long ago passed away. But these books and dozens of other good ones from long ago are still ours to enjoy.

[1]For a free catalog, write Dover Publications, 180 Varick Street, New York, NY 10014.

6

Flights of Fancy

Fantastic Tales Today

This excursion into the preposterous sends us back with renewed pleasure to the actual.

C. S. Lewis
"On Stories"
Of Other Worlds

FANTASY HINTS OF THE GREATER REALITY that lies behind our day-to-day lives, which are mainly made up of scientific fact and ordinary practicality. Such literature often thrusts the reader into new dimensions of space and time, worlds of wonder, and strange powers. Books of fantasy are sometimes gentle, sometimes wild, sometimes humorous, and sometimes deadly serious.

Many authors have praised fantasy. J. R. R. Tolkien calls it the most perfect art form and describes Christ's birth, life, death, and resurrection as the greatest fairy tale of all. And, wonder of wonders, it is true.

G. K. Chesterton said that fantasy reminds us that "the universe is wild and full of marvels. Realism means that the world is dull. . . . In the fairy tales the cosmos goes mad, but the hero does not go mad. In the modern novels the hero is mad before the book begins, and suffers from the harsh steadiness . . . of the cosmos."

C. S. Lewis said, "It would be nice if no little boy . . . were ever at all frightened. But if he is going to be frightened, I think it better that he should think of giants and dragons than merely of burglars."

Even some scientists support the realm of make-believe. Psychiatrists Julius Huescher and Bruno Bettelheim both testify to the beneficial effects of fairy tales and fantasy upon the minds of children. And Albert Einstein once said that the best reading for children is fairy tales, more fairy tales, and more fairy tales.

Whether these tributes to fantasy—and thousands of others—are wise or not, fantasy for children has blossomed in the six decades since World War I, particularly after World War II. These books are exceptionally rich in quality as well as quantity.

This chapter first explores ten of the top children's fantasies in some detail. Then it describes briefly the works of twenty other especially good fantasy writers of the period since World War I. Finally, it lists over fifty other worthwhile writers and some of their work.

TEN TOP CONTEMPORARY FANTASIES

1. DOCTOR DOLITTLE STORIES by Hugh Lofting (1920)

Lofting, who served in the front lines in World War I,

hated to tell his family what he was experiencing. So, being disturbed by the treatment of animals that were used in the war, he made up happy animal stories and sent them to his children in the United States.

After the war, he put the letters together and hesitantly submitted them to a publisher. They were accepted and became *The Story of Doctor Dolittle.* Two years later, the second book, *The Voyage of Doctor Dolittle,* won the Newbery Award. At one point after that, Lofting tired of the continuing series and quit, leaving Doctor Dolittle on the moon. But pressure forced him to write more—twelve in all.

In the first book Doctor Dolittle is offending his human patients because he has too many pets. His one last human patient suggests that he should become an animal doctor. His pet parrot convinces him to do just that and teaches him animal language. This new profession is challenging: it takes a much brighter person to treat animals than to treat humans.

Hugh Lofting has been criticized recently for a kind of benign racism and national chauvinism. Africa's Prince Bumbo begs to be turned white, and King Koko is often pictured sucking a lollipop. Most readers remember that Lofting wrote fifty years ago and overlook these lapses. He was, like most of us, a product of his own culture and did not see beyond it at all points.

2. WINNIE-THE-POOH by A. A. Milne (1926)

One of the pleasures of parenthood is reading Pooh books to children. Their lyrical quality and colorful description are as fascinating as the adventures of one "silly old bear," Winnie-the-Pooh, who is especially fond of eating honey.

Winnie-the-Pooh was written for A. A. Milne's small son Christopher Robin—fondly called Billie Moon—who wished to hear stories about his toy animals.

A child's natural love of cuddly, stuffed animals and his desire to make them live pervade Milne's narrative. He describes Pooh's friends—Piglet, the melancholy donkey Eeyore, Rabbit, Kanga, and Baby Roo—and tells of Pooh's attempts to catch a Heffalump, track a woozle, and his discovery of the North Pole.

A sequel, *The House at Pooh Corner* (1928), contains further adventures and introduces a new friend, Tigger.

Alan Alexander Milne was educated at Cambridge University and served as assistant editor of *Punch* magazine before World War I. His stories are sunny and simple, full of good-natured affection and light humor.

3. THE HOBBIT by J. R. R. Tolkien (1937)

John Ronald Reuel Tolkien was born to English parents in South Africa, was bitten by a tarantula when he was a toddler, and learned to read when he was three. His father died the next year when he, his mother, and baby brother were visiting relatives in England.

When Tolkien was twelve, his mother also died. But he won various scholarships and became a philologist—always learning, studying, and even inventing languages.

In the early 1930s this scholar of language, literature, and mythology wrote a story to read to his sons after supper. One of his ex-students told an editor about it later, who decided to publish it. That forced Tolkien to finish *The Hobbit*, which was published in September, 1937, reviewed enthusiastically in *The Times* by C. S. Lewis, and sold out before Christmas.

The Hobbit tells of the harrowing but humorous adventure of Bilbo Baggins, a homey creature who is tricked into embarking on a dangerous quest to rescue stolen treasure from Smaug the Dragon and becomes a hero because of his simple virtues.

The publisher wanted Tolkien to write another hobbit book right away. He had a huge book, *The Silmarillion*, which he had been working on all his adult life; but that had no hobbits, and the publisher didn't want it. So Tolkien began another hobbit story, but it soon became related to *The Silmarillion* (which was never published until 1977). Instead of being ready in one year, as planned, it grew to a half-million words in thirteen years of writing and was finally published in 1954-1955 in three volumes as *The Lord of the Rings*. It would never have been finished without Lewis's encouragement and prodding.

The Lord of the Rings, which brought to our world new realms of myth, is largely about Frodo Baggins, Bilbo's heir, and his quest. It was not, in Tolkien's opinion, cheerful enough to be suitable for children. The publisher brought it out half reluctantly, expecting it to sell only a few thousand copies.

As publication day neared, Tolkien said, "I have exposed my heart to be shot at." But the favorable responses outweighed the attacks. Sales and interest rose steadily until 1965, when popularity exploded in the United States. By the end of 1968 about three million copies had been sold.

The Hobbit can be read to children as young as five, and *The Lord of the Rings* can be enjoyed by children as young as twelve. In 1976 a new book for very young children came out: *The Father Christmas Letters,* a selection of illustrated story-letters that Tolkien wrote to his children for over twenty years. They tell of Father Christmas's annual adventures with his helper the North Polar Bear.

4. THE NARNIAN CHRONICLES by C. S. Lewis (1950)

Like J. R. R. Tolkien, Clive Staples Lewis was first a brilliant child whose boyhood was shattered by bereavement, then a student at Oxford University, later a professor of literature there, and, eventually, a great writer for children as well as adults. Unlike Tolkien, Lewis was an atheist and an agnostic until conversion to Christianity—with some help from Tolkien—when he was thirty-two.

The Christianity in Tolkien's books is inherent but never obvious. In contrast, the Christianity in Lewis's books often shines through very clearly. Ironically, Lewis was an enthusiastic reader and reviewer of Tolkien's fantasies, but Tolkien did not like Lewis's books for children at all.

A scene that gave rise to *The Lion, the Witch and the Wardrobe* first popped into Lewis's head when he was seventeen. All his fiction sprang from pictures in his mind. But he was in his forties before he tried building a story around it. Then in 1949 he suddenly wrote the whole story with Aslan the golden Lion at its center.

He thought that was all. But in 1950, when this first children's book was published, he wrote *Prince Caspian, The Voyage of 'The Dawn Treader'*, and *The Horse and His Boy* in one year! Then came the last three, published one a year. The final book, *The Last Battle,* won the Carnegie Award for 1956. Lewis received many letters begging for more tales of Narnia, but he said that there were only seven. He died seven years later on the same day President Kennedy was assassinated.

67

The Lion, the Witch and the Wardrobe tells how four English children stumble into the marvelously beautiful world of Narnia, where talking animals are wrongly ruled by a white witch until Aslan overthrows her. *Prince Caspian,* the least popular of the series, tells how the children return a year later to find that many centuries have passed and that the rightful prince needs their help. *The Voyage of 'The Dawn Treader',* tells of a dangerous trip to the end of that world. *The Horse and His Boy* flashes back to the time of the first book and tells of a great adventure that happened during the children's first visit. In *The Silver Chair,* two children seek a captive prince and find much more. *The Magician's Nephew* carries two children back to the creation of Narnia. *The Last Battle* brings the children and all of Narnia to and beyond death in a way that few if any authors could match.

Critic Roger Lancelyn Green said of the chronicles, " . . . they have a fourth dimension, that of the spirit. More than almost any other children's books, they have at their best this kind of reality, and this it is which gives them their quality of vividness, and makes them leave behind an echo and a taste that do not fade."

The Chronicles of Narnia are enjoyed by children as young as six and are good for reading aloud. But many bookstores keep them in their adult fantasy and science fiction section because they have enjoyed overwhelming popularity with college-age people in the 1970s. Older children who are mature readers will also enjoy *Out of the Silent Planet* and *Perelandra,* two of Lewis's three science fiction novels for adults.

5. CHARLOTTE'S WEB by E. B. White (1952)

Elwyn Brooks White was born in 1899 in Mount Vernon, New York. After serving in World War I, he joined the staff of the *New Yorker* and met and married a former editor. In 1929 White coauthored a book with fellow humorist James Thurber called *Is Sex Necessary?*, a satire on popular psychoanalysis. In 1938 his family moved to a farm in Brookline, Massachusetts, where he has lived ever since.

When *Charlotte's Web* was published in 1952, it received unusual acclaim from reviewers and critics in both adults' and children's sections of important literary magazines. Since then it has sold three million hardback copies and has been reprinted by Britain's prestigious Puffin Books six times in six years.

All this public affection is for the humorous but heart-gripping story of a spider named Charlotte who saves the life of a fat little pig named Wilbur by spinning words of praise about him into her web. It is a barnyard fantasy about good country people and the loyalty of animal friends—a story, in one sense, of human strengths and weaknesses and mortality.

White's other books for children are *Stuart Little* (1945), about a mouse who is not just a mouse but the child of human parents, and *The Trumpet of the Swan* (1970). Both books are funny but serious.

6. THE GREEN KNOWE BOOKS by Lucy Boston (1954)

Lucy Boston first became a writer in 1954 when she was over sixty years old!

She was born to wealthy Puritanical parents in England who discouraged pleasure and beauty. When she was 23, she saw an old farmhouse called the Manor at Hemingford Grey in the English countryside.

Boston spent many years in Europe painting. Twenty-four years later she returned to England and bought that manor house. She became obsessed with the house and spent years removing various remodeling jobs that had been added through the centuries. The original walls she uncovered were made of mortarless blocks of stone three feet thick, dating back about eight hundred years.

After twelve years of living in this historic house, and loving it, Boston began to write about it to express that life and love. In her fiction she calls the house Green Knowe. Her son Peter illustrated her books.

Critic and author J. R. Townsend claims that Boston is unsurpassed by any English children's writer and rivalled by only one, Philippa Pearce. Boston herself says that she would like to remind adults of the obsolete concept of joy and to encourage children to use and trust their senses.

In her first two books, *The Children of Green Knowe* (1954) and *The Treasure of Green Knowe* (1958), a small boy named Tolly stays with his great-grandmother, Mrs. Oldknow. There he finds the children who lived in her house three centuries ago. Sometimes he only sees them in a mirror, but other times he talks to them, moving back and forth in time. In *The Treasure of Green Knowe,* blind Susan and her servant friend Jacob appear to Tolly from the eighteenth century.

A young refugee from Burma—Ping—appears in three of the later books, *The River at Green Knowe* (1959), *Stranger at Green Knowe* (1961), and *An Enemy at Green Knowe* (1964). It was *Stranger at Green Knowe* that won the Carnegie Award. Who would have dreamed that a story about a gorilla who escaped from a zoo could be so tender, so evocative, and so exciting?

Lucy Boston has also written *The Castle of Yew* (1965), *The Sea Egg* (1967), *Nothing Said* (1971), *Memory in a House* (1973), *The Fossil Snake* (1976), and *The Stones of Green Knowe* (1976).

7.   TOM'S MIDNIGHT GARDEN by Philippa Pearce

In contrast to Lucy Boston, Philippa Pearce intended to be a writer from childhood on. She was the youngest of four children of a very successful flour miller and corn merchant. She grew up in a large seven-bedroom home, Mill House in Great Shelford, England, near Cambridge.

After college, Pearce spent thirteen years as a scriptwriter and producer in the School Broadcasting Department of BBC. In 1951 she contracted tuberculosis and spent a summer in a Cambridge hospital, longing for her parents' home five miles away on the river. After her recovery she decided to try her hand at setting children's stories in the old home, which was so vivid in her mind. The river is the setting for her first book, *Minnow on the Say* (1955), and the old house and its garden appear in *Tom's Midnight Garden*, with an extra upstairs added for Mrs. Bartholemew.

Critic John Rowe Townsend says that *Tom's Midnight Garden* is as close to being a perfectly constructed book as any he knows. Tom has to stay with his Uncle Alan and Aunt Gwen in their apartment in an old converted house while his brother is quarantined with measles. The landlady, Mrs. Bartholemew, lives at the top of the building. Unhappy Tom sets out to check the old grandfather clock on the ground floor one night when it strikes thirteen. He finds his way into a garden at the back of the house, a garden which is certainly not there when he checks the next day.

This garden belongs to the house and its past, and Tom enters the past through it each night. He is invisible to all the people who inhabit the garden except for a little girl named Hatty. Time passes more quickly in the past, and as Tom visits Hatty each night, she grows up. On the last night of Tom's visit, he learns that Old Mrs. Bartholemew is his friend Hatty and that she has been dreaming him into her own past life.

This masterpiece gives children a concept of the continuity of generations as well as a sense of wonder.

8. WHERE THE WILD THINGS ARE by Maurice Sendak (1963)

Although Sendak is included in the chapter on picture books, he is mentioned here because of his significance as a writer of fantasy. His books are for small children, but they are so significant as true fantasies that they warrant special recognition.

Maurice Sendak is an American of Polish descent born in 1929 and reared in New York. As a child, he read lots of comic books and went to lots of movies—the great "super-escape." He despises schools and claims to be mainly self-educated.

Although he is of Jewish background, he loves the German language and all things German, including *Grimm's Fairy Tales.* A bachelor, he currently lives and works at home in Ridgefield, Connecticut.

Where the Wild Things Are won the Caldecott Medal in 1964. Some people complain that the book is too frightening for children, but the opposite seems to be true. Children love the monsters that are encountered and ruled by Max, the angry little boy who sails away and doesn't come back until his supper appears.

Higglety Pigglety Pop!, subtitled *There Must Be More to Life* (1967), is a nonsensical but tender story about a dog who feels that having everything is not enough. *In the Night Kitchen* (1970) is the story of Mickey, who fell through the night, was baked in a cake where he made an airplane out of bread dough and flew to the Milky Way, dived into a giant milk bottle, and provided milk for the morning cake, ending up asleep in his bed. *The Nutshell Library,* which came out in 1962, is made up of four diminutive books including *Pierre,* a rhymed cautionary tale with a happy ending.

All of Sendak's fantasies for little children have happy endings

9. THE OWL SERVICE by Alan Garner (1967)

Garner was born in 1935 in England, and for many years was too ill to attend school, suffering spinal and cerebral meningitis, diptheria, pleurisy, and pneumonia. He attended Oxford University and studied classics, becoming an expert linguist, but then abruptly dropped out of academic life to devote himself to fiction.

Garner now lives in two houses that stand side by side on top of a prehistoric site. One of his houses was a medieval apothecary shop that was about to be demolished. Garner moved it himself, timber by timber, twenty miles to its present location.

Garner claims he does not write for—but about—children; all his children are really Alan Garner. He says his writing is an act of forgiveness to those people who hurt him as a child. His powerful writing is only for adults and older children who are mature readers.

The Owl Service takes place in a haunted valley in Wales and is based on an old Welsh legend of a wife made out of flowers who once betrayed her magician husband. As punishment, she was turned into an owl, Blodeuwydd. The owl's agony breaks out from time to time, twisting the lives of people in the valley.

In this story a wealthy English girl and her stepbrother visit there with their naive parents and two servants, an extraordinary poverty-stricken Welsh boy and his violently bitter mother.

The previous time the owl's ghastly power affected this family line, it ended in death and shattered lives. This time the death, at least, is averted. *The Owl Service* is a fascinating and frightening supernatural tale of the effects of one generation's sins upon another and the merging of identities.

Prior to this book, Garner wrote *The Weirdstone of Brisingamen* (1960), *The Moon of Gomrath* (1963), and *Elidor* (1965). His favorite of his own books is *The Red Shift* (1973), but it is too adult for most teenagers.

10.   EARTHFASTS by William Mayne (1967)

As a boy, Mayne attended Canterbury Cathedral Choir School, the setting for four of his over forty books.

Earthfasts was his first book to include the supernatural. Two scientifically minded schoolboys see strange movements and hear drumming one evening on a Yorkshire hillside. Then a drummer-boy marches out of the hillside—from 1742 into now—carrying a candle that burns with a cold flame. He has been looking for King Arthur's burial place.

After talking with the two schoolboys and seeing his old house, which is still standing, he marches back. Soon there are strange happenings in the area, and one of the two boys disappears.

In *Hill Road* (1968) Mayne has present-day characters visiting the distant past, the opposite of *Earthfasts.*

Mayne says that most people who read his books are adults—"whatever their age."

The previous ten authors and books rank near the top of twentieth century fantasy for children by almost anyone's standards. The following twenty authors, listed in alphabetical order, are also superb in a variety of ways.

TWENTY MORE AUTHORS OF CONTEMPORARY FANTASIES

Richard Adams, WATERSHIP DOWN (1972)

This is a detailed story about rabbits who leave their endangered warren, make their way across enemy territory under the leadership of Hazel, and are drawn into war with a dictatorial warren ruled by General Woundwort. Although the rabbits are much like people, Adams based his story on the behavior of real rabbits as recorded in *The Private Life of the Rabbit* by R. M. Lockley.

It takes some stamina to get through this rewarding book that has been compared, unfortunately, to Tolkien's *Lord of the Rings.*

Adams began telling this story aloud to entertain his two young daughters when he drove them back and forth to Shakespearean plays at Stratford.

Joan Aiken, THE WOLVES OF WILLOUGHBY CHASE (1962)

Daughter of a famous poet, Joan Aiken is called a

first-class lightweight writer. Her books are full of drama, humor, outrageous exaggeration, and imagination. They are set in a past that never existed because she rewrites history. For instance, *The Cuckoo Tree* (1971) tells of a plan to roll St. Paul's Cathedral of London down into the Thames River on rollers.

Aiken's books include *The Whispering Mountain* (1968), which won the Guardian Award in Britain, *Black Hearts in Battersea, Night Birds on Nantucket, All But a Few, A Hap of Fishbones, The Kingdom Under the Sea, Winterthing, A Small Pinch of Weather, A Necklace of Raindrops,* and *Midnight Is a Place.*

Lloyd Alexander, THE PRYDAIN NOVELS (1964-1968)

Alexander is probably the best-known American fantasy writer of the 1960s. His books tell Welsh legends in a modern folktale style. They have strong characterization and humorous dialogue.

The five books in his series are *The Book of Three, The Black Cauldron, The Castle of Llyr, Taran Wanderer,* and *The High King.* The latter won the Newbery Medal in 1969. These books tell of Arawn, Lord of Annuvin, and the forces of evil, which are defeated by Taran and the Sons of Don. In the end Taran marries the princess and becomes the High King.

Alexander has also written a picture book, *The King's Fountain,* illustrated by Ezra Jack Keats.

John Christopher, THE WHITE MOUNTAINS TRILOGY (1967-1968)

Christopher wrote science and adult fiction before

turning to children's literature. He is an excellent storyteller whose books deal with human problems. This trilogy has been highly popular with both children and critics.

The trilogy is made up of *The White Mountains, The City of Gold and Lead,* and *The Pool of Fire.* In these stories the world is ruled by masters from another planet. These rulers enforce their rule by capping the inhabitants, a kind of mental castration. A few uncapped men struggle to overthrow the rulers, who think of them as lower creatures, before the rulers succeed in changing the earth's atmosphere to benefit only themselves.

Christopher has followed these books with a second trilogy made up of *The Prince in Waiting, Beyond the Burning Lands,* and *The Sword of the Spirits.* Other books of his include *The Guardians* and *The Lotus Caves.*

Helen Creswell, THE PIEMAKERS (1967)

This English author who has taught children and worked for the BBC lives in the country with her husband and daughter.

The Piemakers, her first memorable book, is a mock-heroic account of the Roller family of Danby Dale, telling how they fulfilled the challenge of the king by creating the largest pie in the history of the world—a pie of epic grandeur. Both *The Piemakers* and *The Signposters* are set in a jolly and charming England of the indefinite past. Her other books include *Butterfly Chase, Up the Pier, The Night Watchman, The Bongleweed,* and *A Game of Catch.*

Susan Cooper, THE GREY KING (1975)

Cooper, an English writer who now lives in the United

States, has written a series of five fantasies set in Cornwall and Wales. In this series, supernatural evil is rising, and ordinary mortals along with those who are immortal join the battle between dark and light. The secret son of King Arthur, a boy who lives in our day instead of the past, plays a part in the mysterious and powerful struggle. The titles are *Over Sea, Under Stone; The Dark Is Rising; Greenwitch; The Grey King,* which won the Newbery Award in 1976; and *Silver on the Tree.*

Roald Dahl, CHARLIE AND THE CHOCOLATE FACTORY (1964)

Dahl was born to Norwegian parents in Wales. He was a World War II hero in East Africa; and after the war he became a very successful writer of adult short stories, publishing often in the *New Yorker* magazine. He married Academy Award winning actress Patricia Neal, and they and their four children live in England.

Dahl happens to love chocolate. His sweet tooth paid off. *Charlie and the Chocolate Factory* has sold over a million copies in the United States and was voted the most popular children's book in England, winning over *The Lion, the Witch and the Wardrobe,* which came in second.

This is the story of a poor but virtuous boy who finds the fifth and final golden ticket in a candy bar wrapper and gets to tour Willy Wonka's Chocolate Factory. The other four winners are spoiled and selfish children who disappear one by one, leaving Willy to win the final prize.

Not all critics think this is a good book. One calls it a "thick rich glutinous candy-bar of a book . . . nauseating." Some readers charge that the happy black Oompa-Loompas who work in the factory are a belittling caricature of African pygmies.

Dahl began receiving about five hundred letters a week from children all over the world asking for another Charlie book, so he wrote *Charlie and the Great Glass Elevator,* which included a ridiculous American president and therefore is not part of some libraries' collections. Dahl had in mind all American presidents except his two favorites and says that he disapproves of the super-patriotic respect children are taught to give to the president and the government. His earlier book is *James and the Giant Peach,* and a later book is *The Magic Finger.*

Peter Dickinson, HEARTSEASE (1969)

Dickinson is an editor of *Punch* magazine in England and an author of adult mysteries who turned to children's fiction late in the 1960s.

His three books *The Weathermonger, Heartsease,* and *The Devil's Children* all take place in an England of the near future, in which all machines have been outlawed, the weather is controlled by magic, and ignorance and intolerance are on the increase. In *Heartsease* a couple of English children who have not been caught in the strange national enchantment find a victim of the local hysteria—a young American who was taken for a witch and left for dead by violent villagers. They save his life and help him escape on the tugboat called *Heartsease.* Brotherhood and love are strong values in these books.

William Pene Du Bois, THE TWENTY ONE BALLOONS (1947)

Pene Du Bois grew up in France and won the Newbery Award in his adopted country of America. He illustrated Roald Dahl's *The Magic Finger.*

This is the story of the last days of Krakatoa Island. Professor Sherman sets off in a balloon to see the world and lands on the island to find a civilization that lives on solid diamond. The inhabitants are skillful inventors of amazing gadgets, including a machine for escape should the volcano erupt—which it does, and they escape.

John Gardner, GUDGEKIN THE THISTLE GIRL AND OTHER TALES (1976)

Contemporary adult novelist and short-story author John Gardner has written three farfetched, not-quite-slapstick, fairy tale books for children, somewhat in the James Thurber tradition. There is plenty of magic, with a very light touch and a hint of good-natured satire. Gudgekin, the heroine of one of the stories, is perhaps a parody of Cinderella. In the end she gets what she deserves, which is a handsome prince and a dose of healthy respect for herself and others. The two other books are titled *Dragon, Dragon* and *The King of the Hummingbirds and Other Tales.*

Roger Lancelyn Green, OLD GREEK FAIRY TALES (1958)

R. L. Green has devoted most of his life to children's literature. He read voraciously as a child, home from school much because of illnesses. At the University of Oxford he wrote his thesis about Andrew Lang, the great fairy-tale collector. Green has served as a schoolmaster, dealer in rare books, actor, and college librarian.

In addition to his books for adults, some of which are about children's authors, he has written or edited about thirty books for children. Two of them, *The Luck of the*

Lynns (1952) and *The Theft of the Cat* (1954), take place in his own home, Poulton-Lancelyn, the manor where his ancestors have lived for nine hundred years.

Besides creating his five children's novels, editing *The Complete Fairy Tales of Mary De Morgan* and *The Diaries of Lewis Carroll,* and writing *The Story of Lewis Carroll* and *Kipling and the Children,* Green has served children especially well by retelling *The Adventures of Robin Hood, King Arthur and His Knights of The Round Table, Myths of the Norsemen, The Tale of Troy, Tales of Ancient Egypt, Tales of the Greek Heroes,* and other collections of legends, myths, and folktales that are part of our heritage. Reading his authoritative and detailed renderings of these old fantasies not only enriches children, but enables them to respond more adequately to many contemporary fantasies that refer to the older stories readers are expected to know.

Old Greek Fairy Tales is especially unusual because Green has engagingly retold sixteen Greek myths, stripped of the difficult names and pseudo-historical relationships that usually encumber them. Thus children can learn the basic stories much as they were first enjoyed in ancient Greece.

Robert Heinlein, PODKAYNE OF MARS (1963)

Heinlein has written many extremely popular books on interspace travel. They are good for beginning readers of science fiction as well as more seasoned ones because he is technically accurate but not difficult. Heinlein seems to be well-versed in mathematics, astronomy, and space technology.

He uses both boys and girls as heroes. In *Podkayne of Mars* a sixteen-year-old girl is kidnapped on a stopover at

Venus during her first trip to Earth. Some of his other juvenile science-fiction books are *Rocket Ship Galileo, Have Space Suit–Will Travel, Space Cadet, Starman Jones,* and *Citizen of the Galaxy.*

Norton Juster, THE PHANTOM TOLLBOOTH (1961)

Juster is a practicing architect by profession. In his major book, a bored boy named Milo finds himself traveling through Dictionopolis and other strange lands to save the lost princesses Rhyme and Reason. With his newfound friends, a watchdog named Tock and a genuine Humbug, he braves many obstacles—the Doldrums, a Point of View, the Valley of Sound, the Isle of Conclusions, Digitopolis, and the Mountains of Ignorance. In the process he becomes a better boy. The book is an outrageous *tour de force* full of wordplay and ideaplay, a kind of rollicking cautionary tale.

Robert Lawson, RABBIT HILL (1944)

Lawson won both the Caldecott and the Newbery Awards within five years. As a boy he never tried his hand at art until he decided to enter a poster contest in high school and won first prize. After serving in France in World War I, he became an advertising artist until the Depression temporarily ruined the advertising business.

Fortunately, Lawson was hired to illustrate a book at that time and so discovered his true calling. He published his own first book *Ben and Me* in 1939, the story of Ben Franklin told by his pet mouse Amos. *Mr. Revere and I* (1953) is the story of Paul Revere told by his horse. *Rabbit Hill* and its sequel *The Tough Winter* (1954) foster a tender interest in small wild animals, such as those that surrounded Lawson's own country home, Rabbit Hill. Lawson's fictitious animals are all individual personalities who think and talk a great deal but do not, of course, wear clothes.

Ursula Le Guin, A WIZARD OF EARTHSEA (1968)

Le Guin, an American, has been compared to Tolkien and Lewis because she too has created another world. Earthsea is like Earth in some ways, although it is made up of archipelagos. It lacks machines but has magic. Every village has its local second-rate sorcerer, and high magic is taught at the central university of wizardry.

An evil magician named Ged increases in power and lets loose a nameless evil, which he himself cannot control. It roams, and he eventually has to meet it head on in an unforgettable confrontation.

A Wizard of Earthsea was the first in a trilogy. The other two books are *The Tombs of Atuan* (1971) and *The Farthest Shore* (1972).

Madeleine L'Engle, A WRINKLE IN TIME (1962)

L'Engle was the only child of a well-to-do writer, was educated mainly in Europe, went into drama, married an actor, raised a family, and lives in Manhattan most of the time.

A Wrinkle in Time is a spiritual science-fiction story about the young heroine Meg Murry, her precocious little brother Charles, and their friend Calvin. They rescue Meg's father, a scientist, from the great brain that controls the zombie population of Comazotz. Three good witches—angels—named Mrs. Who, Mrs. Which, and Mrs. Whatsit assist the children in their triumph over evil. *A Wrinkle in Time* won the Newbery Award in 1963, and L'Engle published a sequel, *The Wind in the Door* (1973).

Andre Norton, DARK PIPER (1968)

This is a rather grim science-fiction story in which pirate bands roam the skies after intergalactic civilization crumbles. The last humans on a certain planet—a group of children and young people—are rescued by taking refuge underground with their leader Griss Lugard, who is a latter-day Pied Piper. Lugard and one of the children die, and the rest are left to face life on the abandoned planet. It is strong stuff but well written and full of invention.

Andre Norton used to be a children's librarian in Cleveland, Ohio. She studies folklore, history, anthropology, religion, and archaeology for background information for her books, hoping to entice young people into learning more about subjects she introduces.

Mary Norton, THE BORROWERS (1952)

Mary Norton is English and had a career as a Shakespearean actress long before becoming a popular writer. *The Borrowers,* her original contribution to English folklore, are tiny people who live in hidden places in quiet old country houses. They take their names from the large objects near their homes—such as a clock, a chest, or a harpsichord—and they "borrow" permanently from the house's large occupants.

In *The Borrowers* a boy who visits in the country discovers them and does some borrowing on their behalf—until the exterminator arrives. Norton tells more about the doughty borrowers in other books including *The Borrowers Afield, The Borrowers Afloat,* and *The Borrowers Aloft.*

Her first children's book, which became *Bed-knob and Broomstick,* grew out of stories she told her own children.

James Thurber, THE WONDERFUL O (1957)

This famous American humorist from Columbus, Ohio, was a staff member of the *New Yorker* most of his career. His wistfully inept cartoons, droll anecdotes, and satire made him extremely popular with adult readers. Thurber gradually lost his long battle against blindness and reportedly spent his last years in some emotional as well as physical darkness.

His first book for children was *Many Moons* (1943), the story of a king who tried to get his daughter the moon. Only the jester knew how to succeed.

The Wonderful O is made up of humor and word play. When pirates totally eliminate the letter *O* from the island of Ooroo, all sorts of amazing consequences follow. Finally goodness returns, full of *O*'s, and the moral is clearly spelled out at the end of the book.

His other books include *The White Deer,* a spoof about enchantment, and *The Thirteen Clocks,* a traditional fairy tale in extravagantly playful English.

P. L. Travers, MARY POPPINS (1934)

Pamela Travers spent her childhood in rural Australia buying one-penny books of fairy tales and soaking up her parents' love for Ireland and mythology. Her love for fairy tales has increased with age, and she believes that collectors, anthropologists, and (worse yet) psychoanalysts try to dissect and drain them, but that their meanings cannot be exhausted.

Mary Poppins herself slides up banisters and sails through the air with an umbrella. She is a nursemaid who was brought to the Banks family by an east wind and leaves by a west wind. However, she returns in several sequels including *Mary Poppins Comes Back, Mary Poppins in the Park,* and *Mary Poppins Opens the Door.*

The only objection to these books is that when Mary Poppins visits the United States she meets some Southern blacks who are silly stereotypes, and to many people today that is no longer funny. In fact, it never was.

OVER FIFTY OTHER RECOMMENDED FANTASY WRITERS

Atwater, Richard and Florence, *Mr. Popper's Penguins* (1938)

Beagle, Peter, *The Last Unicorn* (1972)

Bianco, Margery Williams, *The Velveteen Rabbit* (1926)

Bond, Michael, *A Bear Called Paddington* (1960)

Bond, Nancy, *A String in the Harp* (1976)

Cameron, Eleanor, *The Wonderful Flight to the Mushroom Planet* (1954)

Clark, Arthur C., *Dolphin Island* (1963)

Clark, Pauline, *The Return of the Twelves* (1964)

Coatsworth, Elizabeth, *The Cat Who Went to Heaven* (1930)

Colum, Padraic, *The Golden Fleece* (1962) (reissued); *Children of Odin* (1962) (reissued); *The Arabian Nights; Tales of Wonder and Magnificence* (1964) (reissued)

De La Mare, Walter, *Collected Stories for Children* (1947)

Donovan, John, *Family* (1976)

Druon, Maurice, *Tistou of the Green Thumbs* (1958)

Eager, Edward, *Half Magic* (1954)

Erwin, Betty, *Who Is Victoria?* (1973)

Estes, Eleanor, *The Witch Family* (1960)

Farjeon, Eleanor, *The Little Bookroom* (1955)

Farmer, Penelope, *William and Mary* (1974)

Field, Rachel, *Hitty, Her First Hundred Years* (1929)

Fleischman, Sid, *The Ghost in the Noonday Sun* (1965); *McBroom's Ear* (1969)

Garfield, Leon, *The Restless Ghost; Three Stories* (1969)

Godden, Rumer, *Impunity Jane* (1954)

Graves, Robert, *Greek Gods and Heroes* (1960); *The Siege and Fall of Troy* (1963); *Two Wise Children* (1966)

Gregorian, Joyce, *The Broken Citadel* (1975); *Castledown* (1977)

Harris, Rosemary, *The Moon in the Cloud* (1970)

Hughes, Ted, *The Iron Man* (1968)

Janeway, Elizabeth, *Ivanov Seven* (1967)

Jansson, Tove, *Finn Family Moomentroll* (1965)

Jarrell, Randall, *The Animal Family* (1965)

Kendall, Carol, *The Gammage Cup* (1959)

Lightner, Alice, *The Galactic Troubadours* (1965)

Lindgren, Astrid, *Pippi Longstocking* (1950)

Lively, Penelope, *The Ghost of Thomas Kempe* (1973); *A Stitch in Time* (1976)

Masefield, John, *The Midnight Folk* (1927)

McKillip, Patricia, *The Forgotten Beats of Eld* (1974)

North, Joan, *The Light Maze* (1971)

O'Brien, Robert C., *Mrs. Frisbee and the Rats of NIMH* (1971)

Oldenburg, E. William, *Potawatomi Indian Summer* (1975)

Picard, Barbara Leonie, *The Odyssey of Homer* (1952); *The Iliad of Homer* (1960); *The Lady of the Linden Tree* (1962); *Hero Tales of the British Isles* (1963)

Rodgers, Mary, *Freaky Friday* (1972)

Saint-Exupery, Antoine de, *The Little Prince* (1943)

Salten, Felix, *Bambi* (1931)

Sandburg, Carl, *Rootabaga Stories* (1922)

Selden, George, *The Cricket in Times Square* (1960)

Sharp, Margery, *The Rescuers* (1959); *Miss Bianca Stories* (1962)

Silverstein, Shel, *The Giving Tree* (1964)

Sleigh, Barbara, *Carbonel: The King of the Cats* (1957)

Slobodkin, Louis, *Spaceship Under the Apple Tree* (1967)

Stockton, Frank, *The Bee-man of Orn* (1964) (reissued)
Stolz, Mary, *Belling the Tiger* (1967)
Storr, Catherine, *Marianne Dreams* (1958); *The Chinese Egg* (1975)
Wakefield, S. A., *Bottersnikes and Gumbles* (1967)
White, T. H., *Mistress Marsham's Repose* (1946); *The Once and Future King* (1958)
Williams, Ursula Moray, *The Moon Ball* (1967)
Wrightson, Patricia, *The Nargun and the Stars* (1974)

This chapter has mentioned over eighty writers of fantasy for children since World War I. Many of these fantasies are too mature for a very young reader, but none are too young for a very mature reader. C. S. Lewis said once, "I now enjoy the fairy tales better than I did in childhood: being now able to put more in, of course I get more out." He believed that readers who truly enjoy fantasies "for adults" are apt to enjoy fantasies "for children." Fantasies for children and those for adults have much more in common, he thought, than either has with realistic fiction.

7

Realistic Fiction and Biography

Story-telling, as I see it, is a recreating of life, a breathing of life into plausible characters and of facing honestly every naturally occurring situation those characters meet.

Ivan Southall
A Journey of Discovery:
on Writing for Children

REALISTIC FICTION DIFFERS from fantasy in that it must stay within the bounds of what ordinary people consider possible. This is not necessarily the views of advanced spiritual or scientific thinkers—which is often the fabric of fantasy—but what is ordinarily found in school textbooks, however distorted or untrue that might be.

For instance, as recently as 1957, a college psychology textbook entitled *Childhood and Adolescence* was teaching that as soon as children are old enough to read on their

89

own, their tastes differ. Boys like adventure and heroism; in contrast, girls like stories about home, school, and romance. Boys develop an interest in world events; girls limit their interest to home and neighborhood. Boys are quick to enjoy informative literature; girls prefer fiction. Furthermore, boys like funny stories, but girls don't!

People who were once children might well claim that the men who wrote this textbook were off into a bit of fantasy. Simple observation would have corrected them. But their point of view was acceptable enough to be considered realistic in 1957. Likewise, realistic fiction and biography is that which is in step with its time.

Authors of this fiction come from a broad spectrum of society, and their writing reflects their widely varying experiences and ideologies. There is much more variety in children's fiction today than ever before—which, with some unpleasant exceptions, is a good thing for children.

Since World War I this gigantic body of literature consists of animal fiction, historical fiction, contemporary life, adventure and mystery, social and personal problems, and biography. This chapter will describe a few examples in each category, beginning with seven of the many animal stories published between 1926 and 1962, in order of their publication.

ANIMAL STORIES

Smoky, the Cow Horse, by Will James, won the Newbery Medal in 1927. A cowboy story written in loping vernacular, it is about a little range colt whose stubbornness is broken by Clint, a man who becomes his friend.

Twelve years later, Marjorie Kinnan Rawlings wrote *The Yearling* for adults. Some children love it. Jody is a poor lonely boy in the Florida wilds. His love and happiness with his young pet deer Flag is shattered by the harsh realities of poverty: Flag must be shot. This is an extremely sad story that deals with the relationship of a boy and his father under stress.

Lassie Come Home (1948) by Eric Knight is the story of a collie dog who makes a journey from Scotland to Yorkshire, England, to rejoin her master.

Ten years after *Lassie Come Home,* Meindert De Jong wrote *Along Came a Dog,* and Maurice Sendak illustrated it. In this story, a dog befriends and saves the life of a crippled little red hen and is itself finally accepted by the man who tried to get rid of it. De Jong's *Shadrach* (1953) is about Davie and a black rabbit. There is disappointment and anxiety, but even more joy. De Jong has written many stories about animals and children. He won the Newbery Medal for *The Wheel on the School* (1954), also illustrated by Sendak.

Sheila Burnford wrote a critically-acclaimed book, *The Incredible Journey* (1961), about two dogs and a cat who heroically travel two-hundred and fifty miles across the Canadian wilderness to their home. Some consider this book a modern classic.

The same year produced a book already mentioned—Lucy Boston's *A Stranger at Green Knowe* (1961), one of the most wonderful and beautiful stories ever written. This Carnegie Award winner concerns a gorilla named Hanno and a boy named Ping—one displaced from Africa, the other from Asia—caught in a world of concrete floors. The excitement of their meeting and sharing a brief adventure together before the sad but heroic ending is unforgettable.

Philippa Pearce, one of the best writers for children in the English language, wrote *A Dog So Small* (1962), which explores not only our love for animals but also the relationships between three generations and the relationship of imagination to reality. Poor little Ben is promised a dog by his grandfather, but it turns out to be a flat needlework picture. Ben invents a live dog so small he can only see it with his eyes shut. While watching his dog, he is run down in the street. The story comes to a happy but not at all simplistic conclusion, which includes a real live dog.

HISTORICAL FICTION

This type of fiction can imaginatively describe historical events or just tell stories set in some historical period. Either way, the details should be as accurate as possible. Descriptions of fifteen books follow again in order of their publication.

American writer Laura Ingalls Wilder's eight *Little House* books began with *Little House in the Big Woods* (1932) and concluded with *These Happy Golden Years* (1943). Told as fiction, they cover the author's life from four to eighteen as her family moved from Wisconsin to South Dakota in the late nineteenth century. Happiness for the Wilders was not in material possessions but in everyday hardships and successes, family love and activity.

The family comes close to starvation in *The Long Winter* (1940) when the blizzards, one after another, engulf the little towns on the prairie for months. When winter finally breaks and the train gets through, the family celebrates Christmas—in May.

Carol Ryrie Brink's *Caddie Woodlawn* (1935) is set in Wisconsin in the Civil War period, but the war plays no part in the story, which is about frontier farm life.

92

Among other adventures, high-spirited Caddie develops a friendship with some Indians and helps prevent an uprising. This popular book has been criticized because of lively Caddie's submission to a subdued feminine role as part of her maturation. It has also been noted that Mr. Woodlawn could not have inherited a title in England if he would have renounced America.

Eleanor Estes, an American librarian turned writer, created the Moffat family and wrote three books about them. *The Moffats* (1941), *The Middle Moffats* (1942), and *Rufus M.* (1943). They consist of simple, humorous episodes from the younger children's point of view, set in a small Connecticut town called Cranbury before and during World War I. They are among the most delightful family stories ever written.

Esther Forbes's classic *Johnny Tremain* (1943) is set in Boston during the Revolutionary War. A young silversmith, Johnny gets involved in the rebellion, not by actually fighting, but by carrying messages and gathering intelligence. Forbes's excellent description gives one the feeling of being present at the events.

Robert McClosky's *Homer Price* (1943) and *Centerburg Tales* (1951) are delightful tall tales of the American Midwest, which include Homer's capturing a robber gang with the help of a pet skunk and a doughnut machine that won't quit making doughnuts.

In contrast to McClosky's hometown yarns, Olivia Coolidge has written a great many historical stories about the ancient world, such as *Egyptian Adventure* (1954) and *People of Palestine* (1965).

One of the best writers of historical fiction for younger children is Clyde Robert Bulla. His *John Billington, Friend of Squanto* (1956) is about pilgrims and can be read by older children who have reading difficulties. Bulla has written several other books in the same straightforward manner.

Rosemary Sutcliff stayed home from school, partly because of a permanently crippling childhood disease. Her mother read good books to her, but she didn't read for herself until she was nine. As a young adult she became a trained artist, who later turned her specially-made painting desk into a full-time writing desk.

She is now the most widely-acclaimed writer of historical fiction for children. Her *Eagle of the Ninth* (1954) is set in the Britain of ancient Rome, as are *The Silver Branch* (1957) and *Lantern Bearers* (1950), which won the Carnegie Medal.

It has been said that her theme is "the light and the dark." The dark is what threatens; the light what is valued and saved. Sutcliff says her books are mostly about fighting men in a man's world. Other Sutcliff books include *Down Wind* (1961), *Warrior Scarlet* (1958), *Knight's Fee* (1960), and *The Mark of the House Lord* (1965).

Ian Serraillier's *The Silver Sword* (1956) describes the journey of three Polish children across Europe in search of their parents who were taken away by the Nazis. Although it is told calmly, it is an intensely exciting story.

Scott O'Dell of Southern California wrote the Newbery Award winner *Island of the Blue Dolphins* (1960), based on the real story of a twelve-year-old Indian girl. She jumps the ship that is removing her tribe from their island and swims ashore to be with her little brother, who was accidentally left behind. Wild dogs kill him, and the story becomes one of her survival, her love and care for the wounded leader dog, and their inseparable companionship. O'Dell said in an interview, "*Island of the Blue Dolphins* was a direct protest against the gun, and the killing of animals and the killing of people."

94

Sid Fleishman writes energetic tales. *Mr. Mysterious and Company* (1962) concerns the Hachett family who give magic shows—hence the title—in small pioneer towns, working their way west. *The Great Horn Spoon!* (1963) tells of a proper English butler who finds himself serving in the middle of the California gold rush.

Hester Burton of Britain writes novels of social concern. *Time of Trial* (1963), which won the Carnegie Medal, tells of a brave seventeen-year-old girl who gets imprisoned for speaking out for social reform. Burton says that her main interest is the story of young people cast into dreadful trouble who get out of it on their own.

North to Freedom (1965) by Anne Holm (translated from Danish) is the story of a boy of twelve who escapes from a Communist prison camp in Eastern Europe, which is all he has ever known, and journeys alone and ignorant through Europe to find his mother in Copenhagen. It is a heroic, emotional, and heart-warming story, one set in the very recent past.

K. M. Peyton of Britain wrote the Flambards Trilogy about a brave, resourceful young woman named Christina. The time is before and after World War I. The titles are *Flambards* (1967), *The Edge of the Cloud* (1969), and *Flambards in Summer* (1969). The story includes a once-wealthy English family's decline from aristocratic living, a young man's fatal desire to be a pilot, and Christina's realistic adjustment to completely new responsibilities after the war. This series shows the immense social changes that were taking place in that tumultuous period.

Paula Fox's *The Slave Dancer* won the Newbery Medal in 1973 for telling of a black boy who was kidnapped in 1840 and forced to work on a slave ship, exercising the sick slaves on deck. The ship is wrecked. The boy survives, but the spiritual horror of his journey is unforgettable. One of Fox's earlier books, *How Many Miles to Babylon?* (1967), tells of a small black boy who is kidnapped by older boys, forced to assist them in their dog-stealing racket, and lets the dogs go at night.

CONTEMPORARY LIFE, ADVENTURE, AND MYSTERY

These three topics cover a wide range indeed. Descriptions of only six examples are given here, in order of publication, followed by a discussion of series books.

Arthur Ransome was a well-educated journalist, author, and world traveler long before he wrote and illustrated his first adventure book for children, *Swallows and Amazons* (1930). Because Ransome himself enjoyed boats, fishing, and vacations, he wrote about very capable, very young children who enjoyed these same diversions. There are twelve books in all, describing in accurate and convincing detail all the skills of outdoor living that time, luck, energy, and money can provide. Reading these stories is clearly an exercise in wish-fulfillment for ordinary children who are hampered by protective parents, busy schedules, uncooperative companions, and boatlessness.

Beverly Cleary writes humorously and unpretentiously about third-grader Henry Huggins, his friends, and his dog Ribsy. Henry's highly improbable but very American adventures include *Henry Huggins* (1950), *Henry and Ribsy* (1954), *Ramona the Pest* (1968), and others.

Natalie Savage Carlson's *The Happy Orpheline* (1957) tells about twenty little girls in a dreary orphanage near Paris, where they have amusing adventures. This book and its sequels give a slight acquaintance with France as well as a merry view of communal living.

William Mayne writes at a highly rarified literary level and appeals more to adults than to children, although his books are written for children. His *Swarm in May* (1957) is a mystery set in an English choir school. *A Grass Rope* (1962) won the Carnegie Medal, and *The Battlefield* (1967) deals with some mysterious old carved stones in Yorkshire. For younger children, *No More School* (1965) tells of two girls who keep the village school open unofficially when the teacher is ill. Mayne's books for younger children are, interestingly, among his best.

Madeleine L'Engle's *Meet the Austins* (1960) is one of the last significant family books—at least for the time being—in which the family is intact, loyal, prosperous, and happy. Dr. Austin's household, overflowing with laughter and love, manages to incorporate a spoiled ten-year-old girl whose parents were killed in an accident. *The Moon by Night* (1963) and *The Young Unicorns* (1968) continue the story. This family is superior to ordinary families in culture, talent, spirit, and parental perfection—and aware of their superiority. L'Engle now regrets that she allowed her publisher to water down *Meet the Austins,* making it more sweet and pious than she had intended. She has said, "My feeling is that if a children's book isn't equally or even more enjoyed by adults then it's not worth doing."

Charlotte Zolotow began work at Harper & Row as a young stenographer during the Depression, soon became a children's editor there, and eventually the author of about sixty brief picture books, illustrated by various outstanding artists. She sometimes writes about personal relationships in such books as: *Big Sister and Little Sister* (1966), *When I Have a Son* (1967), *The Hating Book* (1969), and *A Father Like That* (1971). The latter is about a little boy who thinks about what his father might be like if he had one. Zolotow never sets out to preach at children, but she believes in "a reconstruction of an emotional need."

Literary people tend to deplore the fact that the most popular children's books in the area of contemporary life, adventure, and mystery are "pulp" series about intrepid children such as Nancy Drew, mass-produced by "fiction-factories."

Edward Stratemeyer, the creator of *Nancy Drew,* was born in New Jersey in 1862 and read Horatio Alger success stories with a passion. After selling his own story of this genre, he chose his first pen name, Arthur (for author) M. (for a million copies of his future books) Winfield (for success in his chosen field). He went to work for Street and Smith, the greatest dime-novel publishers, and when Horatio Alger died, Stratemeyer had the honor of completing Alger's unfinished books.

In 1899 Stratemeyer dashed off his first three *Rover Boys* stories, which by 1930, when Stratemeyer died, amounted to thirty volumes and had sold 5,000,000 copies. In 1906 Stratemeyer set up his Stratemeyer Syndicate in which he wrote a few books himself and dictated outlines for hundreds and hundreds of others that he hired various writers to complete. After his death, his talented daughters carried on.

Stratemeyer had invented a huge crew of imaginary authors. His chief assistant, Howard Garis, not only helped him to run the company but also "filled in" every single *Tom Swift* and hundreds more. When enthusiastic readers demanded details about one beloved author, May Hollis Barton, the Syndicate obligingly published a fabulous biography of her. She was, of course, really Stratemeyer. So was Carolyn Keene.

The identity of most of the real writers has been kept secret. They were paid $50 to $250 per book and allowed from a week to a month to turn it in. The books were full of exciting adventures from beginning to end, perfectly moral, and utterly devoid of all literary excellence, deep sensitivity, or intellectual enrichment.

They did not go unopposed. Libraries refused to carry them, which only increased sales. The chief librarian of the Boy Scouts of America wrote a tract called "Blowing Out the Boy's Brains," which swept the nation with its warning that these cheap adventure books debauch and destroy boys' imaginations by overstimulation, just as alcohol will debauch and destroy their bodies.

Interestingly enough, when Dr. Robert A. Nisbet of Columbia University, scholar of "intellectual history" and author of many books, was asked in 1977 to list the books that had shaped his life he named a dozen. The first three—one-quarter of a list that also included Alexis de Tocqueville and William James—were: the books of Horatio Alger; the Tom Swift series by Victor Appleton; and the Boy Allies series by C. W. Hayes.

The 1970s has seen a tremendous new pulp-novel trend in hack writing, epitomized by Harlequin Books of Toronto, which publishes twelve new Harlequin romances every month, selling about one-hundred million in the United States in 1977. Besides that, these books account for over a quarter of all paperbacks purchased in Canada. They are silly, old-fashioned love stories.

Harlequin's marketing director claims that 140 women write these books for his company, and that the average purchaser buys seventy-two of their books a year. "Our books are easy to read in that there are no great thoughts involved," he says.

Time will tell if these innocent, low-quality adult books

filter down to pre-adolescent girls. It seems likely. Today their readers are assumed to be bored housewives. But their most famous reader has been Lillian Carter, the president's mother. She admits reading 144 of them every year.

PERSONAL AND SOCIAL PROBLEMS

There have always been books about personal and social problems, but subjects that used to be taboo in children's literature have proliferated since 1960. Some of these books are sensitive and constructive. Others seem to be by uncaring or unskilled writers. In this area knowledgeable parents will want to guide their children's selection. Here are ten authors of personal and social problem books and then some warnings.

Lois Lenski won the Newbery Medal for *Blue Willow* (1939), a book about migrant farm workers and Janey's longing for a permanent home. Lenski followed this with a number of books about disadvantaged regional groups, such as North Carolina mountain people. *Strawberry Girl,* set in Florida's backwoods, won the Newbery Medal in 1946.

Jean Little, a Canadian writer, was born blind. *Mine for Keeps* (1962) is a realistic account of how a young girl with cerebral palsy adjusts to family life after five years at a school for the handicapped. The sequel is *Spring Begins in March* (1966). In *Home from Far* (1965), a girl's twin brother is killed, and then foster children are brought into the home. In *Look Through my Window* (1970) and *Kate* (1971), Jean Little explores growth in family relationships and self-understanding.

Australian Ivan Southall writes of children in stress and danger or under specific handicaps. *Hell's End*

100

(1963) deals with a group of children who return home from a cave exploration with their teacher and discover that their town has been flooded and deserted. *Let the Balloon Go* (1968) deals with a spastic child's heroic efforts at climbing a tree. *To the Wild Sky* (1967) won the Book of the Year Award in Australia.

In *Where the Lilies Bloom* (1965), Vera and Bill Cleaver tell about an extraordinary fourteen-year-old named Mary Call Luther who struggles to control and support her parentless family of four in the Smokies.

Elaine Konigsburg's Newbery Medal winner *From the Mixed-up Files of Mrs. Basil E. Frankweiler* (1967) is a story of two clever children who take up residence in the Metropolitan Museum of Art after running away from home. Her Newbery Honor Book *Jenifer, Hecate, Macbeth, William McKinley, and Me, Elizabeth* (1967) concerns interracial friendship and apprenticeship to a witch. These two winners were her first two books. *(George)* (1970) is the story of an intelligent, likable boy with a schizoid personality. Konigsburg illustrates her own books.

Virginia Hamilton's maternal grandfather was born a slave and ran away from the Kentucky-Tennessee area with his mother. Her grandmother was half Cherokee Indian. In 1975 she became the first black woman and black writer to win the Newbery Medal. She lives with her husband and four children in Yellow Springs, Ohio, where her relatives have lived for several generations.

She has absorbed a great deal of black history and experience, which she transforms into literature. *Zeely* (1967), a book about black dignity, tells the story of a child who is awed by the beauty of a neighbor who looks like a Watusi queen. *The House of Dies Drear* (1968) is a mystery story set in a house that was once a station on the

101

Underground Railroad. *M. C. Higgins, the Great* (1974) won both the Newbery Medal and the National Book Award in 1975. In this unusual book, which is not extremely popular with children, M. C. Higgins, aged thirteen, lives on Sarah's Mountain and spends his time watching. The slag heap poses a terrible danger to his family and makes M. C. long to move away, but moving remains a dream.

Patricia Wrightson's *A Race Course for Andy* (1968) describes a retarded child who believes he owns a racetrack. Wrightson is an Australian writer of great skill.

John Rowe Townsend, long a children's book critic in England, decided to write some books he would like to read and has become a major writer of children's realistic fiction. His *Trouble in the Jungle* (1969) deals with slum children abandoned by adults and their skirmish with criminals. *The Intruder* (1969) tells of a boy who is mystified about his parentage after a stranger claims to be the true son of his mother and father. *Noah's Castle* (1975) is the story of one family that disintegrates during their struggle for survival after the British economy collapses. The country's financial poverty is less than the emotional poverty of the father—who has futilely hoarded for himself and his family—and his collapse is more complete than the country's. Townsend manages to write about catastrophe with courage and to describe a sick personality without rancor. The book is not fantasy because it seems quite possible and is not depressing because of the goodness in some of the young characters.

William Armstrong's *Sounder* (1960), which won the Newbery Medal, is about a black sharecropper's family. The father is jailed for stealing food for his wife and family—a brief but touching story.

Robert Newton Peck's *A Day No Pigs Would Die* (1972) is

a bloody and tender book about a thirteen-year-old Shaker boy whose simple, poverty-stricken father works himself to death as a hog butcher. It is written in rural Vermont vernacular, with warmth and humor. The book describes sex and death vividly but wholesomely. It should be read aloud only by those who are not ashamed to cry. There are powerful lessons here in courage, virtue, and love.

The richly sensual and emotional experience of approaching maturity in *A Day No Pigs Would Die,* the sensitive handling of religious differences, the good-natured tolerance of a little human foolishness, and the sudden awareness of the tragedy of past adultery—these qualities are the opposite of what we find in some of the most popular realistic fiction for children today.

Judy Blume has been considered a daring pioneer who presents the realities of growing up for children who are in fifth and sixth grades. She includes "bad words," wet dreams, masturbation, and peeking at a naked person. She often writes about wealthy New Jersey parents who are, to judge by their incredibly stupid behavior, either mentally ill or alcoholic. The materially spoiled children she describes are neurotically competitive about becoming sexually provocative and are already social climbers in elementary school. There seems to be no feeling for weather, animals, nature, or the rest of the world outside this unpleasant social environment.

Blume takes criticism of her subject matter as a prudish reluctance to be honest with children and help them toward happy sexual adjustment. A mother herself—and a product of affluent New Jersey society— she really aims to guide children as well as entertain them. She happens to approve of the apparently self-centered, impersonal, shallow life-style she writes about.

103

To a sensitive, informed adult these books are bleak stories about bleak lives, and they are depressing. But they are exciting and immensely popular with sixth-grade girls and are widely available in bookstores and public libraries.

Are You There God? It's Me, Margaret (1970) by Blume is often misrepresented as a story of religious tolerance. A standard guide to children's literature mistakenly says, "Margaret is also confused about religion; will she be Jewish like her father or Christian like her mother? She doesn't solve all her problems but does decide that her faith is strong, that she can worship in her own way, whatever her formal affiliation." That is completely false.

In fact, Margaret's inept father has no use for the Jewish faith, and her mother hates and rejects Christianity. Margaret sees her indulgent Jewish grandmother as a bit silly and despises her old "Christian" grandparents, who bear about as much resemblance to Catholics or Protestants as they do to astronauts—one would have to search hard to find a more malicious caricature in children's literature. The preposterous old woman even signs her lying letter to her only daughter, "Your mother, Mary Hutchins," as if her grown daughter didn't know her own mother's name.

There is no indication that Margaret considers the truth and teaching of either faith; she sees religion as a social affiliation and finds public worship a bore. However, she is in the habit of reporting her interests to God occasionally, much as a girl of eleven jots in a diary. For example: "I can't wait until two o'clock God. That's when our dance starts. Do you think I'll get Philip Leroy for a partner? It's not so much that I like him as a person God, but as a boy he's very handsome."

Margaret stops speaking to God when she misses out on a trip to Florida. And she becomes furious at her parents and grandparents for arguing about whether she should have any religion. But when her main desire is fulfilled and she begins to menstruate, she talks to him again: "I know you wouldn't have missed this for anything!"

One peculiar detail in this book, which is preoccupied with menstruation, is the patently false assurance that menstruation is painless. It is now common knowledge that the intense cramping pain experienced by some girls is organic, although many male doctors used to dismiss it as mental.

Blume has every right to endorse Margaret's kind of agnosticism, but it seems a shame that she has done it with disdain for the subject. And it is a shame that her book is falsely represented as a story about tolerance and maturation. Ironically, this book is sold at some conservative Christian bookstores.

Blume's *Forever,* for young teenage girls, describes what it is like to have a first sexual affair, including physical details and clever pillow talk. Pregnancy, venereal disease, and prolonged emotional entanglement are no problem for the socially successful heroine, who feels much more mature after the experience as she steps into a new romance.

If parents are surprised about the books that are approved reading for ten-to-fifteen year olds, they are sure to be more surprised by some that are coming out for children between five and ten. *You Think Just Because You're Big You're Right* is an elegantly designed full-color picture book by Albert Cullum that portrays many little children and their concerns: parents fighting horribly, a little boy and girl caught with their pants down, priggish parents who keep pornography in the bedroom, the opinion that all librarians are prissy fools, a mother who often gets drunk after supper, a little girl whose breasts develop too early, a little girl who sits in the closet with the shoes her father left behind, a little boy whose crazy mother keeps him in a dark room watching TV with her every day, a boy who is locked out of the house after school until a tall man bursts out and almost steps on him as he leaves, a boy caught masturbating, a boy who is afraid of being sent to a psychiatrist. . . . This is a very expensive picture book for little children, meant to sympathize with them in their varying problems. It stops just short of picturing incest and child battering, and offers no hope.

One wonders which little children will receive such a memorable book for Christmas or will read it in a bookstore or library. It probably won't help suffering children very much, but it will disturb some of the others with its high-voltage contents and mind-boggling illustrations.

So long as it sells, realistic children's literature is going to continue to include drugs, divorce, suicide, gang war, crime, rape, the occult, parental adultery, deformities, unwanted pregnancies, racial prejudice, homosexuality, abortion, mental illness, and sick family relationships. It will also continue to include problems of sexual awakening and religious opinion. Some of these books will be constructive and wholesome; others will seem quite unworthy.

Protests to publishers, bookstores, and libraries about specific books should not be made too hastily. It might be wise to become acquainted with similar books, in order to judge which are more or less helpful and which are really pernicious. But reading and discussing these books with your children, if they are going to be exposed to them anyway, would be wise to do.

BIOGRAPHIES

Samuel Johnson wrote over two hundred years ago, "He that writes the life of another is either his friend or his enemy, and wishes either to exalt his praise or aggravate his infamy." Most biographies for children tend to the former, though the best ones avoid an over-sanctification of their subjects.

Biography for children has traditionally differed from biography for adults in that it usually left out scandalous, gruesome, or tragic episodes in the subject's life. Biographies for children also avoid documentation, and they often take greater liberties by casting facts into fictionalized dialogue.

Two very loose kinds of biography are fictionalized biography and biographical fiction, the latter taking even more liberty with fact.

Several weaknesses in the field of children's biographies have been pointed out in the past. For example, the biographical series are usually weak because they contain poor biographies as well as good ones. Two of the better series for beginning readers are the Harper & Row "I Can Read" history books and the Young Cromwell Biographies. The Random House Landmark Books present historical landmarks in American life and indicate reading and interest level. The Cromwell biographies are good for older readers. The Harper & Row Breakthrough Books are good, emphasizing breakthroughs in human achievement. Putnam's Sports Hero Series and an American Hero series—the Horizon Caravel Books—and the American Heritage Junior Library all contain much good biography for children.

Amos Fortune, Free Man (1950), written by Elizabeth Yates, won the Newbery Medal. Yates visited the tombstone of Amos in Jaffrey, New Hampshire, and was inspired to write his biography. Amos was born a prince in Africa. He was sold in Boston, learned the tanner's trade, and eventually purchased his own freedom. He spent the rest of his life buying freedom for other slaves. Yates also wrote biographies of American women of courage—Dorothy Canfield Fisher and Prudence Crandall.

Thomas Jefferson is the subject of numerous biographies. One of the best is by Leonard Wibberly, whose four-volume Jefferson cycle (1964-1966) is done with great care and scholarship. Wibberly stated in 1962, "For how can a book be educational which discourages children from reading? . . . a book which is so thin in characterization, so stilted in its prose, and is so contrived . . . that the young reader goes to it as to a penance."

Theodora Kroeber's *Ishi, Last of His Tribe* (1964) is an exciting book about the last surviving member of the Yahi Indians, who lived at the foot of Mount Lassen in hiding, afraid of being annihilated by white men. One by one they died until only Ishi remained. He left and encountered the white men, who took him in instead of killing him. He spent his last years working with the museum staff of the Museum of Anthropology and Ethnology at the University of California.

COLLECTIVE AND INDIVIDUAL BIOGRAPHIES

The following is a list of ten good collective biographies:
Asimov, Isaac, *Breakthroughs in Science* (1960)

Bontemps, Arna, *Famous Negro Athletes* (1964)
Buckminster, Henrietta, *Women Who Shaped History* (1966)
Daugherty, Sonia, *Ten Brave Men* (1951)
Daugherty, Sonia, *Ten Brave Women* (1953)
Fleming, Alice, *Doctors in Petticoats* (1964)
Fleming, Alice, *Great Women Teachers* (1965)
Kennedy, John, *Profiles in Courage* (1964)
McNear, May and Lynd Ward, *Armed with Courage* (1957)
Sutcliff, Rosemary, *Heroes and History* (1966)

And here are thirty good individual biographies for children:

Bulla, Clyde, *Lincoln's Birthday* (1966)
Bulla, Clyde, *Pocahontas and the Strangers* (1971)
Churchill, Winston, *Joan of Arc* (1969)
Commager, Henry Steele, *America's Robert E. Lee* (1971)
Coolidge, Olivia, *Gandhi* (1971)
Coolidge, Oliver, *Tom Paine, Revolutionary* (1969)
Coolidge, Olivia, *Winston Churchill and the Story of Two World Wars* (1960)
Dalgliesh, Alice, *The Columbus Story* (1955)
Daugherty, James, *Abraham Lincoln* (1943)
Daugherty, James, *Daniel Boone* (1939)
D'Aulaire, Ingri and Edgar Parin, *Abraham Lincoln* (1939)
D'Aulaire, Ingri and Edgar Parin, *George Washington* (1936)
Davis, Russell and Brent Ashabranner, *Chief Joseph, War Chief of the Nez Perce* (1962)
Forbes, Esther, *America's Paul Revere* (1946)
Komroff, Manuel, *Mozart* (1956)
Judson, Clara Ingram, *Abraham Lincoln* (1961)
Judson, Clara Ingram, *George Washington* (1951)
Meigs, Cornelia, *Jane Addams: Pioneer for Social Justice* (1970)
Meigs, Cornelia, *Invincible Louisa: The Story of the Author of Little Women* (1968)
Noble, Iris, *Emmeline and Her Daughters: The Pankhurst Suffragettes* (1971)
North, Sterling, *Young Thomas Edison* (1958)

109

Peare, Catherine Owens, *The Louis D. Brandeis Story* (1970)

Sandburg, Carl, *Abe Lincoln Grows Up* (1928)

Singer, Isaac Bashevis, *A Day of Pleasure: Stories of a Boy Growing Up in Warsaw* (1968)

Spencer, Cornelia, *Sun Yat-sen: Founder of the Chinese Republic* (1967)

Sperry, Armstrong, *John Paul Jones: Fighting Sailor* (1953)

Sterling, Dorothy, *Freedom Train: The Story of Harriet Tubman* (1954)

Washington, Booker T., *Up From Slavery* (1917)

Wibberley, Leonard, *Zebulon Pike, Soldier and Explorer* (1961)

Young, Margaret B., *The Picture Life of Martin Luther King, Jr.* (1968)

This chapter has only been a sample of realistic fiction and biography for children in our time. Many good writers and dozens upon dozens of worthy titles were not even mentioned.

Rhyme and Reason

Poetry, Nonsense, and Information

No book is really worth reading at the age of ten which is not equally (and often far more) worth reading at the age of fifty—except, of course, books of information.

C. S. Lewis
"On Stories"

"IF A MAN WERE PERMITTED to make all the ballads, he need not care who should make the laws of a nation." Eighteenth century essayist Andrew Fletcher may have overstated his cause, but the underlying rationale is often true. Just as the pen is mightier than the sword, so stories often do more for people than statutes, and rhymes can help children as much as rules.

The first author of a book of poems especially for children was the Puritan minister Isaac Watts, who published *Divine Songs for Children* in 1715. His purpose was

111

to teach Christianity to children, and he did it so beautifully that his poems were well-known by children for two centuries. "Cradle Hymn" begins:

> Hush! my dear, lie still and slumber,
>   Holy Angels guard thy bed!
> Heavenly blessings without number,
>   Gently falling on thy head.

Only four years after *Divine Songs*, another book of poems for children was published in London—*Songs for the Nursery, or Mother Goose's Melodies.* There were surely earlier collections of nursery rhymes, but this is the first one on record. And not one copy is left.

In 1744 Mary Cooper of London published at least two volumes of nursery rhymes for sixpence each, called *Tommy Thumb's Pretty Song Book* "for the Diversion of all Little Masters and Misses." They were only three inches tall and less than two inches wide, and the one remaining copy of volume two is a treasure in the British Museum. The first rhyme in the book is one that knowledgeable children still say to ladybugs—in England called ladybirds—when they catch them and let them go unharmed. (The English name "Our Lady's bird" actually means the Virgin Mary's bug and may have been given because ladybugs aid desirable plant life.)

> Lady Bird, Lady Bird,
> Fly away home.
> Your house is on fire,
> Your children will burn.

Perhaps this first line in the oldest remaining nursery rhyme book inspired the name and insignia of one of today's children's publishers: the Ladybird company, located in Loughborough, England. This is the same city in which a conference of contemporary children's writers meets annually at the University's Library School.

Don't assume from "Lady Bird" that *Tommy Thumb's Pretty Song Book* was all sweetness and gentility. The second rhyme is:

Little Robin redbreast
Sitting on a pole,
Niddle, Noddle,
Went his head,
And Poop went his Hole.

Needless to say, all coarse rhymes like that were refined later as adult standards for children's literature became stricter. Other familiar rhymes in that oldest collection include "Sing a Song of Sixpence," "Little Tom Tucker," and "Baa, Baa, Black Sheep."

John Newbery's book of nursery rhymes was published before the Revolutionary War, and the American Isaiah Thomas pirated the edition in 1786. The toddlers of our nation grew up on nursery rhymes from the beginning. There have been hundreds of editions of them, large and small, some with truly beautiful illustrations. *The Annotated Mother Goose* (1962) by Baring-Gould, *The Oxford Dictionary of Nursery Rhymes* (1951), and *The Oxford Nursery Rhyme Book* (1955) by Opie are the most comprehensive editions.

Only recently have advertising jingles tended to take the place of nursery rhymes for little children. But "Mary Had a Little Lamb" is still the most famous verse in the English language!

Next came William Blake's *Songs of Innocence* in 1789, a

collection of artistic poetry. Many scholars say that these poems were intended for children, and his darker *Songs of Experience*, which came five years later, for adults. Some have claimed that both volumes include good poems for children, and other readers say that all of Blake's poems are strictly for adults.

Blake was a controversial genius in his own day, and he still is. He saw angels and other supernatural visitors, and much of his later mystical writing is very obscure. He taught his beloved wife, Catherine, to read and write, and she worked with him on his art and writing the rest of his life. They produced each of his books themselves, with personally made copper engravings of the lettering and designs and delicate water color shading added by hand. Each volume sold for five shillings, but they were not at all popular. Today the few that are left are almost priceless.

One of the favorite poems by William Blake and one of the best suited for children is "The Lamb."

> Little Lamb, who made thee?
> Dost thou know who made thee?
> Gave thee life and bid thee feed
> By the stream and o'er the mead;
> Gave thee clothing of delight,
> Softest clothing, woolly, bright;
> Gave thee such a tender voice,
> Making all the vales rejoice?
> Little Lamb, who made thee?
> Dost thou know who made thee?
>
> Little Lamb, I'll tell thee;
> Little Lamb, I'll tell thee:
> He is called by thy name,
> For he calls himself a Lamb.

114

He is meek, and he is mild;
He became a little child.
I a child, and thou a lamb,
We are called by his name.
  Little Lamb, God bless thee!
  Little Lamb, God bless thee!

To turn from Blake to the next book of poetry for children is almost to turn from the sublime to the ridiculous, but sisters Ann and Jane Taylor were not writing funny verses. Their book *Original Poems for Infant Minds*, published in 1804, was immensely popular, full of sentimental virtue and cautionary verses that warned children to behave. Children no doubt enjoyed the rhymed stories of "Meddlesome Matty" and "Dirty Jim," but the one and only poem that endures today is "Twinkle, twinkle, little star."

Next came a poem for children that has remained a top seller for 150 years!

On Christmas Eve in 1822, Clement C. Moore, a Bible scholar who taught Greek and Oriental literature at an Episcopal seminary in New York, wrote a poem about Santa Claus. He spent a few hours alone in his study and then presented his family with "A Visit from St. Nicholas" or, as it is popularly called, " 'Twas the Night Before Christmas."

A year later he had it published in a newspaper, and soon it swept the country, permanently determining Santa's looks, personality, and *modus operandi* for American children. Moore died forty years later and is remembered today in encyclopedias for that single incredibly popular poem.

At the time of Moore's death, a very serious, gifted, and beautiful English woman brought out a story-poem for children called *Goblin Market.* The author was Christina Rossetti, and the story told of a girl who ate enchanted fruit and almost perished craving for more until she was saved by her loving sister. Today *Goblin Market* is interpreted by Freudians as a thinly disguised account of disappointed love, and it is enjoying revived popularity with some adult readers. Sexual symbolism aside, it seems rather sinister for children, although it is a great work of art. In 1872 Rossetti brought out her collection *Sing Song* for children, which includes delightful verses like this one:

Mix a pancake,
Stir a pancake,
Pop it in the pan;
Fry the pancake,
Toss the pancake,—
Catch it if you can.

This book is still a good choice for little children. Christina Rossetti was a devout Anglican who cited the King James Bible as her main source of poetic inspiration. Some critics consider her the finest female poet that England ever produced. The following lines are often quoted today, even by people who never heard of Rossetti:

What can I give Him,
  Poor as I am?
If I were a shepherd
  I would bring a lamb,
If I were a Wise Man
  I would do my part,—
Yet what I can I give Him,
  Give my heart.

It seems as if Rossetti's poem that begins "Minnie and Mattie/ And fat little May,/ Out in the country,/ Spending a day." must have been the inspiration for the magnificent children's poem that e. e. cummings wrote in the mid-1950s, which begins:

> maggie and milly and molly and may
> went down to the beach (to play one day). . . .

If so, we have even more to thank her for.

Shortly after Rossetti's *Sing Song,* Robert Louis Stevenson brought out what is probably the most famous poetry book for children, *A Child's Garden of Verses.* It came out in 1885 under the title *Penny Whistles.* Stevenson wrote to a friend, "I have now published, on 101 small pages, THE COMPLETE PROOF OF MR. R. L. STEVENSON'S INCAPACITY TO WRITE VERSES."

Instead he has been informally called the "poet laureate of childhood" because of this book. Verses such as "My Shadow" remain a favorite part of many adults' childhood:

> I have a little shadow that goes in and out with me,
> And what can be the use of him is more than I can see.
> He is very, very like me from the heels up to the head;
> And I see him jump before me, when I jump into my bed.

Stevenson began these verses at about thirty, while he wrote *Treasure Island,* and went on writing them for four years, through some serious illness. Ten years after he finished them, he died of a stroke.

The next overwhelmingly popular book of poems for children came almost forty years later: *When We Were Very Young* by A. A. Milne, who also wrote *Winnie-the-*

117

Pooh. Milne composed a little verse about his son Christopher Robin, which was published in a magazine, and he was urged to write more. After he refused, he wondered what the verses would have been like if he had agreed and wrote them anyway. This whimsical book was published in 1924. In 1927 he followed it with *Now We Are Six.* They have both been reprinted hundreds of times in England and the United States.

In his autobiography Milne said, *"When We Were Very Young* is not the work of a poet becoming playful, nor of a lover of children expressing his love, nor of a prosewriter knocking together a few jingles for the little ones; it is the work of a light-verse writer taking his job seriously even though he is taking it into the nursery. It seems that the nursery, more than any other room in the house, likes to be approached seriously."

Walter De La Mare agreed: "I know well that only the rarest kind of best in anything can be good enough for the young." His largest collection of poems for children was published in 1944—*Rhymes and Verses: Collected Poems for Children.* Some readers favor that one, and others favor an early one called *Peacock Pie* (1913). De La Mare was not just a superb verse writer like Milne, but a major poet of the twentieth century, and the only one who concentrated on children's poetry. His work is melodious, finely crafted, and often humorous.

Most people would probably name T. S. Eliot as the most prominent English poet of the twentieth century and one of the most difficult to comprehend. Relatively few realize that he wrote a single book of children's poetry, which does not depend upon his famous name to endear itself to readers.

Eliot had the nickname "Old Possum." He called his book for children *Old Possum's Book of Practical Cats.* It is a zany but dignified collection of stories about cats Eliot claims to have known. All cat and light-verse lovers are happier for meeting them in this book. And children love to hear the preposterous accounts read aloud.

Eliot was an American who moved to England and became British. Two of his contemporaries who stayed in the States never wrote books for children but did make selections of their poems available to children late in their careers. These are *You Come Too* (1959) by Robert Frost and *Wind Song* (1960) by Carl Sandburg.

One of the most prominent American poets for children today is David McCord, who began his career with children in 1952 with his fifteenth book of verses, *Far and Few*. David McCord is not a major poet like Eliot, Frost, and Sandburg, but he has a superb ability to communicate the pleasures of poetry and the fascination of words.

Parents who read poetry themselves will discover wonderful poems for their children occasionally in adult books—such as the poems "anyone lived in a pretty how town" by e. e. cummings, "The Congo" by Vachel Lindsay, and "Narnian Suite" by C. S. Lewis. These three all demand to be read aloud.

There are hundreds of good books of contemporary poetry for children available in libraries. One good way to identify a family's favorite poets is to sample lots of them in a good anthology such as *Time for Poetry* by Arbuthnot and Root.

And for a truly unusual insight into poetry-making, read *The Bat-Poet* (1963), written by Randall Jarrell and illustrated by Maurice Sendak. It is the story of one little brown bat who is stirred by what he sees and hears and then creates evocative poems. "The trouble isn't making poems, the trouble's finding somebody that will listen to them," the little bat observes.

NONSENSE BOOKS

Poetry, even when it is grave, is a kind of word play. Jokes are word play, too, and poetry, jokes, and riddles are related in that way. Some poems are riddles, and some jokes are almost poems. They can be very sophisticated or simple enough for children. Or both. And nonsense is one of the joke forms most often written for children.

The first great hero of nonsense in England was Edward Lear, who was born in 1812 into a large, wealthy family. Edward was a pale, sickly child with twenty sisters and brothers. When Lear was thirteen, their father was thrown into debtors' prison, and the family was suddenly destitute. Edward always suffered from a mild form of epilepsy, which he called "Terrible Demon." He learned to support himself by drawing plants, birds, and animals in detail, and was hired by the Earl of Derby to live at his country estate and draw his collection.

The stifling atmosphere in this aristocratic society made Lear want to act silly. He didn't, of course, but he enjoyed the friendship of the Earl's little grandchildren and started to write limericks, which he illustrated with very silly sketches. Lear published his *Book of Nonsense* in 1846 and *Nonsense Songs and Stories* in 1871.

The greatest master of nonsense was Lear's contemporary Lewis Carroll, who brought out *Alice's Adventures in Wonderland* in 1865. The nonsense in *Alice* is far less random and pointless than it seems; in fact some of it can be comprehended only by mathematicians!

English children in Carroll's day all realized that when the Mad Hatter sang:

"Twinkle, twinkle, little bat!
How I wonder where you're at!"

it was a burlesque on Jane Taylor's five-stanza poem "The Star" from her prim and proper book *Original Poems for Infant Minds*. "The bat" probably referred to Carroll's—(Dodgson's)—colleague with that nickname, whose math lectures were often incomprehensible to students. Of course children didn't know that.

Early in her adventure Alice tried to recite the best-known poem in her day from Isaac Watts's *Divine Songs for Children*, "Against Idleness and Mischief," which was standard memory work:

How doth the little busy bee
   Improve each shining hour,
And gather honey all the day
   From every opening flower!

How skillfully she builds her cell!
   How neat she spreads the wax!
And labours hard to store it well
   With the sweet food she makes. . . .

Her voice came out hoarse and strange, but less strange than the words:

How doth the little crocodile
   Improve his shining tail,
And pour the waters of the Nile
   On every golden scale!

How cheerfully he seems to grin,
   How neatly spreads his claws,
And welcomes little fishes in,
   With gently smiling jaws!

Here the safe and pious Watts poem turned into a bit of chilling savagery. Children loved the switch.

For a much broader sample of Carroll's nonsense for children, turn to *The Book of Nonsense* edited by Roger Lancelyn Green. It even includes some of Carroll's letters to one of George MacDonald's daughters and other assorted nonsense from 50 A.D. to the present.

Other silly books include *The Bad Child's Book of Beasts* by Hilaire Bellock (1896), *Johnny Crow's Garden* by Leslie Brooks (1903), *Tirra-Lirra* by Laura Richards (1932), and *Parents Keep Out* by Ogden Nash (1951). Also there is *Tongue Tanglers* by Charles and Francis Potter, *A Book of Bosh* by Edward Lear and Brian Alderson, *Professor Branestawm's Compendium* by Norman Hunter, *A Book of Milliganimals* and *Silly Verse for Kids* by Spike Milligan, *The Puffin Joke Book* by Bronnie Cunningham, and *The Puffin Book of Improbable Records* by Blake and Yeoman. There are usually lots of jokes and riddle books available for children, and they sometimes entice slow readers.

FACT BOOKS

Books of unusual and amusing facts are also gobbled up, even by immature readers. *The Guinness Book of World Records* fascinates most children sooner or later, and gifted children can get immense pleasure out of browsing in a good dictionary or encyclopedia.

Some books of information are delightful as well as useful. V. M. Hillyer's *A Child's History of the World* (1924) and *A Child's Geography of the World* (1929) are quaint and engaging overviews that have been updated. Even slightly outdated copies are fun to read and painlessly teach much to children that average high-school graduates don't know.

Henrick Willem Van Loon's *The Story of Mankind* (1922), for older and more studious children, was the first winner of the Newbery Medal. Because this is an extremely complex and informative book—compressing the entire history of civilization into one volume—it is a far cry from most of the less daunting Newbery winners that have followed it.

America: A History for Peter (1960) by Gerald W. Johnson is a handsome three-volume set in large clear print that tells the story of the United States for Mr. Johnson's grandson Peter. The book titles are *America Is Born, America Grows Up,* and *America Moves Forward.* They are sensible, readable, and beautifully illustrated. Most adults could profit from reading them.

Ladybird now offers over three hundred and fifty little hardback books of fifty pages, full of colored pictures, that cover everything from *Julius Caesar and Roman Britain* to *Magnets, Bulbs and Batteries.* These books are not great works of art or literature, but they pack an amazing amount of well-organized information into a small space with large clear type and very low prices![1]

MAGAZINES AND INEXPENSIVE BOOKS

The most beloved children's magazine in the United States today is *Ranger Rick's Nature Magazine,* which boasts a million readers. Although it features beautiful color photos and easy-to-read information about all kinds of animal life, it also includes charts, maps, jokes, puzzles, projects, poems, letters, and stories.[2]

Another superb informative magazine for children is *World,* which is a little sister of *National Geographic.* Typical issues have contained lavishly illustrated articles on the details of King Tut's treasure, motocross racing, beavers and penguins, underwater music, and the pinhole camera—with a real cardboard camera included and directions for its use![3] *World* is a winner of the Golden Lamp Award for excellence in educational journalism.

England has a magazine designed to give children information about some of the authors they enjoy. It is *Puffin Post.*[4]

Puffin Books is unique among children's book publishers, because, under the leadership of Kaye Webb, it has been dedicated to bringing the best books to children at the lowest possible prices. To read a current Puffin catalog of over seven hundred titles and descriptions is a delight in itself.

Kaye Webb says, "It is true, and easy, to say that Puffin's aim is to publish 'the very best in children's reading,' but less easy to define exactly what *is* the best, since what proves exactly right for one child can evoke no response in another . . . we believe that even if no other books were available, you would find here a sufficient variety of the very best that has been written to supply your children with 'sufficient imaginative nourishment to draw on for a lifetime.' "[5]

Kaye Webb happens to be on the editorial board of *Cricket,* the beautiful American magazine-book for children that includes poetry, nonsense, information, and fiction, new and old.[6]

And so the circles close and spirals turn. Poetry merges through fantasy into nonsense, and the flip side of nonsense is information. Children's books sail across the Atlantic and sail back again.

It was the great American poet Emily Dickinson who gave children the lines:

There is no frigate like a book
To take us lands away . . .

We order and ship the books, but books are our ships and order us. We carry our books, and our books carry us. We read the books, and the books read us. Writers mold the books, and books mold the writers.

That sounds like nonsense. It is fact. . . . and a kind of living rhyme.

[1]For a free illustrated catalog, write Ladybird Books, Ltd, Loughborough, Leicestershire, England. Most of their books can be ordered by mail from Leicestershire Learning Systems, Box 335, New Gloucester, Maine 04260.

[2]*Ranger Rick,* National Wildlife Federation, 1412 Sixteenth Street NW, Washington, DC 20036.

[3]National Geographic *World,* Department 00277, 17th and M Streets NW, Washington, DC 20036.

[4]The Puffin Club, Dept. A, Penguin Books Limited, Harmondsworth, Middlesex UB7 ODA, England.

[5]For a current Puffin book list, write to Penguin Books at the address above or to either of the following bookstores: The Children's Book Centre, 229 Kensington High Street, London W2, England, or The Red House Book Shop, 93 High Street, Thame, Oxon, OX9 3HJ, England. Those stores can advise Americans who want Puffin books how to order and purchase them by mail, since few are imported into the United States.

[6]*Cricket,* Open Court Publishing Company, 1058 Eighth St., La Salle, IL 61301.

9

Open Eyes

Picture Books and Illustrations

*And what a book it was! . . . so beautiful that Lucy stared at it for
a whole minute and forgot about reading it. The paper was crisp
and smooth and a nice smell came from it; and in the margins,
and round the big coloured capital letters at the beginning of
each spell, there were pictures. . . . And the longer she read the
more wonderful and more real the pictures became.*

C. S. Lewis
The Voyage of 'The Dawn Treader'

ONE OF THE MOST OVERWORKED CLICHES is "a picture
is worth a thousand words." Taken literally, the total
worth of that famous quotation itself would be .007 percent of a snapshot. In fact, the magnificent phrase "In
the beginning God created the heavens and the earth . . ."
would be worth .01 percent of somebody's sketch of said
event. That shows how silly it is to force a false competition between words and pictures.

Common sense tells us that both words and pictures
are capable of ranging from sublime to wretched. Their

forms and functions are obviously different. A blind person finds pictures useless and depends upon words. A color-blind person—at least 5 percent of our boys are partially color-blind—misses some of the value of colored pictures. And a person suffering from aphasia, the inability to use words, may not understand words and may value pictures highly. Most people, however, find the combination of words and pictures a double delight.

Some books have no illustrations at all, some happen to have illustrations, and others depend upon their illustrations. The latter are called picture books.

The first real picture book for children was translated into English in 1659. It was called *The Visible World,* by a monk named John Amos Comenius, and was strictly informative. A recent equivalent is our contemporary giant, *The Random House Encyclopedia,* which includes 11,000 color pictures and is very entertaining for children to browse in, although it is a sad excuse for a reference book because its scholarship is so thin and uneven. (In the same price range, *The Columbia Encyclopedia* is a superb choice for a family reference book that includes maximum worthwhile information. But it has no room for pictures.)

Between *The Visible World* and *The Random House Encyclopedia,* technology has changed picture books and illustrations radically. Color printing—in place of hand-painted water coloring—was beginning by the time Queen Victoria took the throne in 1837 and improved greatly by 1865.

The first three great color picture-book artists were Walter Crane (1845-1915), Randolph Caldecott (1846-1886), and Kate Greenaway (1846-1901)—all born just as Hans Christian Andersen's *Fairy Tales* was being translated into English.

Walter Crane produced over thirty meticulously designed books for preschoolers. He was a master of decoration and design. He wrote:

> There is at least one great advantage in designing children's books: that the imagination is singularly free, and let loose from ordinary restraints, it finds a world of its own, which may be interpreted in a spirit of playful gravity . . . It appears to me that there is a certain receptive impressionable quality of mind, whether in young or old, which we call child-like. A fresh direct vision, a quickly stimulated imagination, a love of symbolic and typical form, with a touch of poetic suggestion, a delight in frank gay colour, and a sensitiveness to the variations of line, and contrasts of form—these are some of the characteristics of the child, whether grown up or not. Happy are they who remain children in these respects through life.

Caldecott was in some ways the best artist of the three. He is remembered for the sixteen children's books he illustrated before his untimely death at age forty. His illustrations had more zest, humor, and energy than those of Crane and Greenaway; he often included bits of the English countryside and vivid action. It is in memory of him that Americans have named their highest award for children's illustration.

Like Caldecott, Kate Greenaway produced sixteen books, and she was the most popular of the three. She owed her phenomenal success to the fine publisher Edmund Evans, an old friend of her father. He was already the successful publisher of Crane and Caldecott when she took her first collection to him.

When he saw her gracefully sentimental pictures of clean, happy, decorous children dressed in beautiful old-fashioned clothes from her own imagination, he immediately accepted them and soon published 20,000 copies of her first book, *Under the Window.* That was an extremely large printing for a book that was in no way inexpensive. But it wasn't large enough. Before Evans could issue a second printing, copies of the first were reselling at inflated prices!

Kate Greenaway's style was sweet and serene. She was, in fact, a kind of costume designer. Clothing manufacturers used many of her original ideas, and there is a Kate Greenaway brand of children's clothing in the United States today. Furthermore, some of her books are still in print.

In a private letter Kate Greenaway once exclaimed, "Things *are so* beautiful and wonderful, you feel there must be another life where you see more—hear more—and *know* more. All of it cannot die."

She wrote insignificant poems to go with her drawings, and in one of them she said, "When I am dead and all of you stand round and look upon me, my soul flown away ... what beauteous land may I be wandering in ...?" She died, unmarried and childless, in 1901: the very year that Beatrix Potter, the next of the greatest picture-book artists, surprised the world with *Peter Rabbit.* Her life and picture books were described in chapter five. But excellence of her drawing is one reason for her success.

Crane, Caldecott, Greenaway, and Potter were all English. The most distinguished American illustrator for children up to this time was Howard Pyle, who liked to write and draw about idealized historical romance set in England or Europe. Two of his art pupils became excellent American children's illustrators—Jessie Wilcox Smith and N. C. Wyeth, the father of America's favorite artist Andrew Wyeth and grandfather of contemporary artist Jamie Wyeth.

Meanwhile, Arthur Rackham (1867-1934) was pursuing his career as a children's illustrator. He illustrated the original edition of *Peter Pan in Kensington Gardens* and literally dozens of other major children's books. He was a superbly gifted artist whose merging of the real with the fantastic resulted sometimes in scenes of cozy innocence and other times in grotesquely terrifying creations. He was one of the first illustrators to really take advantage of the new possibilities in color halftone printing. Rackham understood the technicalities of the new process and used his colors to create profound moodiness and mystery.

Three outstanding contemporaries of Arthur Rackham were the brothers Charles and William Heath Robinson and Edmund Dulac. Fantasy and fairy tale paintings by all four of these men are still unusually rich and elegantly beautiful.

A publishing company in San Diego, California, has undertaken to make the works of these four men and others available today. In their catalog they say:

> The pictures in old children's books have an enormous power. Partially it originates in their importance within our history. We, in seeing them, are made to know again that glorious moment when we first entered the kingdom of books. Secondly, the pictures are often magnificent. The artists, in painting and drawing for children, were cut free of earth's bonds. The medium is a liberating one, inviting those who work within it to unleash their invention, to give shape to the dreams otherwise unrealized![1]

A cartoonist for *Punch*, Ernest Shepard, illustrated all of Milne's *Winnie-the-Pooh* books, for which he is most famous. He even surpassed Rackham with some of his illustrations for *The Wind in the Willows*. Most of

Shepard's work was pen and ink, but when he was eighty he produced eight full-color pictures for the Golden Anniversary Edition of this famous book. Be sure to borrow that 1959 edition from the library. His daughter Mary Shepard illustrated *Mary Poppins*.

Jean de Brunhoff was a French painter who had sons four and five years old. They told their father how much they liked the story of a little elephant that their mother had made up for them. The father began to illustrate the story for his sons and soon found himself creating a large handwritten book, *The Story of Babar*. It was published right away, in 1931, and became immensely popular in England and the United States.

Jean de Brunhoff completed five more Babar books before he died in 1937, when his son Laurent was only twelve. Laurent de Brunhoff, who lives in Paris, went on with his father's series as soon as World War II ended, adding more than twenty new titles. They sell by the millions. As critic Emma Fisher has observed, Babar has changed from an innovation to an institution. Babar has recently been accused of racism, and he has often been analyzed for his political and social ideals.

Poor King Babar can also serve as an example of the decline of book quality. When the original set came out in the 1930s, the average life span for books was fifty years.

Today Babar books are produced much more modestly; the extra touches of quality have been gradually eliminated. Worse yet, the quality of book paper has declined so in the last twenty-five years that books published today will probably turn yellow and fall apart in less than fifty years, according to Library of Congress experts.

Unless some new chemical preservation methods are eventually developed, today's children's books cannot be guaranteed for future generations. Books by artists such as Edward Ardizzone, first winner of the Kate Greenaway Medal, will have to be reissued someday in order for them to continue to exist. Ardizzone was born in Vietnam in 1900 to an Italian father who was a citizen of France. However, he was reared in England and is thoroughly British. He won the Greenaway Medal in 1956 for his book *Tim All Alone.* He began this series of books about Tim by telling and retelling them to his own children. (He is now a grandfather many times over.) Although he lacked opportunity for much art training, he is now a famous watercolor artist, has taught art at the Royal Academy in London, and has illustrated more than one hundred and sixty books!

Ardizzone, who loves the Authorized Version of the Bible, says that when he was thirteen someone gave him a pocket edition of *Pilgrim's Progress,* illustrated with many tiny engravings. The vividness of Bunyan's writing and those little engravings crystalized his own desire to become an illustrator and painter. Many years later he got to illustrate *Pilgrim's Progress* himself. He claims that children have no taste in art and will enjoy both good and bad books. "All the more reason, therefore," he says, "that we should give them the best."

A more recent winner of the Kate Greenaway Medal is Pauline Baynes, who won it for the elegant children's reference book *A Dictionary of Chivalry* in 1969. This book by Grant Uden took Baynes more than two years to complete because of the wealth of its detail that is typical of her delicate precision, lyrical linear quality, and devotion to accuracy. She has recently illustrated a series of nature books in color. Although she has illustrated over sixty books, she is best known in the United States for her illustrations of the Narnian Chronicles.

Garth Williams is one of America's most familiar illustrators. He drew the perfect pictures for *Charlotte's Web,* Laura Ingalls Wilder's *Little House* books, and Carlson's *Orpheline* stories. For all his success and honors, he never happened to win the Caldecott Medal. That is one of life's ironies.

In contrast, Robert McCloskey has won the award twice and was the first artist to do so. He won it for *Make Way for Ducklings* in 1942 and then for *Time of Wonder* in 1958.

Richard Scarry is a picture-book creator who does not receive much praise from critics. But his merry books are so cherished by children that they often fall apart from overuse. These "educational" books are full of droll animal-people with preposterous activities and almost endless visual detail, all in good fun.

Scarry is an American who now lives in Switzerland, but wants it understood that he is loyal to his homeland and pays his full income taxes. His first and biggest success was *Best Word Book Ever,* which has sold over a million copies in the United States and is published in many other countries as well. Scarry crams as much as he can into every page; his basic motivation is fun. He has fun, children have fun, and the parents who tape the books back together have fun.

Ezra Jack Keats won the Caldecott Medal for his first book, *The Snowy Day.* His warm, simple stories about black children living in the inner city take place in a moving array of colors and textures that are sheer visual delight. His book *Skates!* was so popular in Japan that it led to the opening of a roller skating rink in Tokyo, where he was the guest of honor.

Later a Japanese mother wrote to tell him that her little boy so cherished his autographed copy of that book that after he was killed in a traffic accident she placed it in his coffin. Keats took that as the highest kind of tribute.

OTHER NOTABLE PICTURE BOOKS

There are dozens and dozens of excellent children's illustrators today, because it is an attractive field for the finest of artists. Here is a list of some other notable picture books—either for excellence or for enduring popularity:

Story of Little Black Sambo (1899) Helen Bannerman
Raggedy Ann and Andy (1924) Johnny Gruelle
Millions of Cats (1928) Wanda Gag
Ferdinand (1936) Robert Lawson
Mike Mulligan and His Steam Shovel (1939) Virginia Lee Burton
The Country Bunny and the Little Gold Shoes (1939) Marjorie Flack
Madeline (1939) Ludwig Bemelmans
Stone Soup (1947) Marcia Brown
The Biggest Bear (1952) Lynd Ward
The Happy Lion (1954) Roger Duvoisin
Chanticleer and the Fox (1958) Barbara Cooney
Swimmy (1964) Leo Lionni
Sylvester and the Magic Pebble (1969) William Steig
Frog and Toad Are Friends (1970) Arnold Lobel
The Circus (1970) Brian Wildsmith
Snow White and the Seven Dwarfs (1972) Nancy Eckholm Burkert
Alexander and the Terrible, Horrible, No Good, Very Bad Day (1972) Ray Cruz
Lion and Blue (1974) Fleur Cowles
Ashanti to Zulu: African Traditions (1976) Leo and Diane Dillon
The Bear Who Wanted to Be a Bear (1977) Jorg Muller

THE MASTER ILLUSTRATOR

There is one children's artist today who is generally

134

hailed as the greatest—Maurice Sendak. Critic John Rowe Townsend says that Sendak is not only a fine illustrator of books that do not depend upon pictures, but he is the greatest creator of picture books since color publication evolved well over a century ago.

Sendak was born in Brooklyn in 1928 to parents who had come to America before World War I from small Jewish towns outside Warsaw. The father worked in New York's garment district. His three children considered him a wonderful storyteller, elaborating on tales he had heard in his own childhood. Sendak looks forward to writing one of his father's stories when he feels ready.

Up to the age of six Sendak spent much of his life sick in bed, and he thinks that this intensified his strong feelings about physical objects, including books. Later he and his brother, who was five years older, spent time making books together. While still in high school, he had a part-time job with All American Comics working on "Mutt and Jeff" comic books.

After high school Sendak worked for a window display company for a couple of years and then constructed window displays for a New York toy store, taking a little art instruction at evening school.

He was discovered by Ursula Nordstrum, children's editor at Harper & Row in 1950, the year that our new surge of fantasy began. In only two years he became prominent in his chosen field with *A Hole Is to Dig*. From then on he was in great demand. Among the more than fifty books he has illustrated, the *Little Bear* series is especially loved. In 1956 Sendak published the first of the few books he has written himself, *Kenny's Window*.

Sendak is largely self-taught. He is an ardent admirer of Randolph Caldecott. Another artist who has influenced him is the mystic William Blake (1757-1827), author of "The Lamb." Sendak is touched by Blake's poetry as well as his art. Blake was a genius. Sendak may be one also.

A former art critic for the *New York Times* claimed that Sendak is "one of the most powerful men in the United States" because he "has given shape to the fantasies of millions of children—an awful responsibility." The writer must have been assuming that the peculiar potency of Sendak's work makes a deeper and more lasting impression than the rest of the images and ideas that barrage children daily.

Sendak says, "If I have an unusual gift, it's not that I think I draw particularly better or write particularly better than other people (I've never fooled myself about that); rather, it's that I remember things other people don't recall—the sounds and feelings and images of particular moments in childhood. It seems my child-self is still alive and active."

He says of *Where the Wild Things Are,* "Max is my truest and therefore my dearest creation."

PICTURE STRIP BOOKS

One of Sendak's more recent and less significant books is *Some Swell Pup* (1976), which is entirely in comic strip form. To be honest about picture books and illustrations for children, one has to admit that ordinary comics are the most popular picture books of all.

The very year that gave us *Alice's Adventures in Wonderland,* 1865, marked the beginning of comic strips and comic books, for "Max and Moritz" by Wilhelm Busch appeared in Germany in that year. "The Yellow Kid" first appeared in the *New York World* on February 16 1896, and since then comic strips have become a staple of

America's reading diet. About twelve million drawings have been done for comic strips. They have produced such fictitious celebrities as Little Orphan Annie, Barney Google, the Katzenjammer Kids, Blondie, Superman, Donald Duck, Batman, and finally in 1950, the Peanuts children.

Between 1963 and 1969 alone, there were 36,000,000 copies of eighteen different Peanuts books printed. There were also two books by Robert Short, *The Gospel According to Peanuts* and *The Parables of Peanuts,* pointing out the Christianity in these strips.

But during this same period, risque Marvel comics came to appeal to college students. Underground comics enjoy immense popularity with all ages and significantly influence younger children. *Zap* is a prominent example of this genre, strongly anti-establishment and blatantly sexual.

Mad magazine was a satirical comic book ruled out by many parents and teachers in the 1960s because its audacious style caused people to assume it, also, was against traditional values and blatantly sexual. Dr. Vernard Eller of La Verne College in California exonerated *Mad*'s readers when he demonstrated in his book *The Mad Morality* that this magazine was in fact attacking immorality and supporting the Ten Commandments all along.

Parents will do well to hope that *Mad* does not change its morals, because—whatever its art quality—more children read *Mad* in a year than read Caldecott Medal winners in a generation.

[1]The Green Tiger Press, 7458 La Jolla Blvd., La Jolla, CA 92037.

10

Recordings and Recording

'Grandmother dear, what big ears you have!'
'The better to hear you with, my child!'

"Little Red Riding Hood"
Perrault's Fairy Tales

READING SILENTLY IS ONE THING. Reading aloud is another. Listening to someone read aloud is quite different again. And listening to a recording of someone else reading is a different thing altogether. It puts more people and more technology between the book and the listener. The live reader is the middleman between the author and the audience. The recorded reader becomes a plastic middleman, but a very valuable one.

What a wonder it is when the author of a beloved book tells us the story in a recording. Charles Dickens and

138

Mark Twain, for example, used to add to their income by reading or reciting their works to crowded theaters full of enthusiastic listeners. They were superb readers and entertainers. But there was no way to record their voices.

Vachel Lindsay, who lived from 1879 to 1931, used to travel about the American Midwest giving readings of his poetry when recording was still a crude art. There is one weak, scratchy-sounding album of his old reading performances—hearing it makes clear why he was in demand. His bold, rhythmic, explosive rendition makes his poems come alive as he intended. Once we have heard his oral version, the printed poems take on more of his tone and pacing.

James Weldon Johnson, whose life began a few years before Lindsay's and ended a few years after, was a teacher, lawyer, musician, American Consul in South America, and secretary of the National Association for the Advancement of Colored People. He is remembered primarily now for *God's Trombones* (1927), a series of poems in the tradition of vigorous black sermons, rich in imagery. He was a magnificent reader and recorded these brilliantly on 78-rpm records. America will be the richer if they are reissued in a contemporary 33-rpm album. Children would especially enjoy the poem-sermon "The Creation." In the meantime, one prominent Los Angeles preacher has passed Johnson's poetry off as part of his own sermon writing and has sold cassette tapes of it as well!

Carl Sandburg made many recordings, including his book *Rootabaga Stories,* which comes in three albums. In at least one family, the children listened to his rolling renditions so often that as young adults they would still quote whole passages back and forth when something set them off. Sandburg also recorded his short stories for children, "The Five Marvelous Pretzels" and "The Three Nice Mice Brothers," along with a collection of his children's poems, which begins with his explanation of what poetry is. His Peter Potato Blossom Wishes says, "And you have to listen close up with your ears and be nice when you are listening." No one can read Sandburg better than Sandburg.

Across the Atlantic, no one could read Dylan Thomas better than Thomas himself. His "Child's Christmas in Wales," "Reminiscences of Childhood," "The Visit to Grandpa's," and "Quite Early One Morning" bring his childhood alive. They are fascinating, especially if one gets a printed version to better understand the humor and beauty in the waterfalls of words that seem to thunder from him.

Frank O'Connor's two short stories about his Irish childhood, told in his own clear but colorful Irish brogue, "My Oedipus Complex" and "The Drunkard," might be enjoyed by older children as well as parents (who will want to listen to them first because families vary in their standards of propriety). The latter tells how the bored little boy samples and drinks his father's two pints of ale after a neighbor's funeral and becomes sick, disgracing himself and his father. Thus he accidentally achieves his heart's desire—to save his parents from one of his "teetotalling" father's drinking sprees. Both stories are told with tenderness and good humor.

J. R. R. Tolkien wasn't easy to understand sometimes in personal conversation, because he would drop his voice low, or get excited and run his words together. But he had a flair for drama. Fortunately, there is an album available in which he reads the riddle chapter from *The Hobbit.* The title of the album is *J. R. R. Tolkien Reads and Sings His* The Hobbit *and* The Fellowship of the Ring.

Furthermore, his son Christopher has produced a recorded reading from *The Silmarillion,* but this is not of interest to many children.

Once one has fallen in love with *Old Possum's Book of Practical Cats* with its droll illustrations, what better pleasure than to hear these story-poems read aloud in a very dignified British style by T. S. Eliot himself. One can't hear his eyes twinkling, but one is sure of it.

Ogden Nash's humor is farther beyond the comprehension of children, but there are probably some of his preposterous verses that they would enjoy hearing him read with his proper Boston accent. He recorded an entire album of them.

In England for many years there has been a daily story program for children on BBC television called "Jackanory." The title came from the old nursery rhyme:

I'll tell you a story of Jackanory;
Now my story's begun.
I'll tell you another of Jack and his brother,
And now my story's done.

This program has included classics of English literature, all kinds of stories from all over the world, original new fiction, and true stories from any time. The readers range from famous actors to people who are unknown but have something special to share. Some "Jackanory" stories are available in records.

Children who are old enough and sturdy enough to not be disturbed by the horror in Edgar Allan Poe can hear renditions by Basil Rathbone. In fact, many children might enjoy Rathbone's reading of the poem "The Raven," even if Poe's short stories are above their fear threshold.

141

Boris Karloff, another actor noted for frightening people, has recorded much literature for children, including Kipling's *Just So Stories* and *Jungle Book*, Kenneth Graham's *The Reluctant Dragon,* and *Stories of Sherlock Holmes.* Both Boris Karloff and Michael Redgrave have read Hans Christian Andersen stories on record albums.

OTHER RECORDED READINGS

Here are thirty of the hundreds of notable recorded readings for children, listed alphabetically by their readers' last names:

Allen, John, *Oliver Twist* by Charles Dickens
Bacall, Lauren, *The Thirteen Clocks* by James Thurber
Begley, Ed, *Tom Sawyer* and *Huckleberry Finn* by Mark Twain
Bloom, Claire, *Dick Whittington and His Cat and Other English Fairy Tales* retold by James Reeves
Bloom, Claire, *Goldilocks and the Three Bears* by Robert Southey
Bloom, Claire, *Heidi* by Johanna Spyri
Brennan, Walter and Brandon de Wilde, *Stories of Mark Twain*
Channing, Carol, *Madeline* by Ludwig Bemelmans
Harris, Julie, *Little House in the Big Woods* by Laura Ingalls Wilder
Harris, Julie, *The Story of Scheherazade* from *The Arabian Nights*
Harris, Julie, *Stuart Little* by E. B. White
Harris, Julie, and Richard Kiley, *Heroes, Gods and Monsters Of the Greek Myths* rewritten by Bernard Evslin
Kitt, Eartha, *Folk Tales of the Tribes of Africa* from various sources

142

Leigh, Vivien, *The Tale of Peter Rabbit* by Beatrix Potter
LeGallienne, Eva, *The Velveteen Rabbit* by Margery Williams
Ludwig, Salem, *Short Stories of Mark Twain*
McKenna, Siobhan, *Irish Fairy Tales* from various sources
Nesbit, Cathleen, *Jason and the Golden Fleece* from *Tanglewood Tales* by Nathaniel Hawthorne
Pettingell, Frank, *A Christmas Carol* by Charles Dickens
Quayle, Anthony, *The Adventures of Robin Hood* retold by Paul Creswick
Quayle, Anthony, *Aladdin and His Lamp* from *The Arabian Nights*
Quayle, Anthony, *Ali Baba and the Forty Thieves* from *The Arabian Nights*
Quayle, Anthony, *The Exploits of Don Quixote* retold by James Reeves
Quayle, Anthony, *The King of the Golden River* by John Ruskin
Redgrave, Michael, *Gulliver's Travels* by Jonathan Swift
Ryan, Robert, *The Red Badge of Courage* by Stephen Crane
Sorel, Guy, *The Three Musketeers* by Alexandre Dumas
Tandy, Jessica and Hume Cronyn, *Wind in the Willows* by Kenneth Grahame
Verdon, Gwen, *The Story of Ferdinand* by Munro Leaf

Furthermore, every year Newbery Award Records issues a recorded dramatized and abbreviated version of that year's winner.

And the American Bible Society sells excellent recordings of the Bible to the public at very low prices.[1]

Families may find a special need for recorded literature if they like to do handwork, if there is illness and a need for restful entertainment, if there is a visual or reading comprehension problem, or if parents are unable to read to their children as often as they would like.

But families without these special needs are also apt to have a few favorite recordings that they treasure and turn to from time to time. Many libraries have excellent collections of both phonograph albums and cassette tapes. They can also provide patrons with the names and addresses of outlets where these items can be ordered. Cassette tapes have the advantage of portability, and cassette players are so common today that this is an excellent way of listening to good things while moving about the house, traveling in the car, or occupying evenings on a trip.

FAMILY RECORDINGS

Families who own cassette players can, of course, make their own recordings. One family asked their two grandmothers to tell tales from their childhood, youth, and child-rearing years on cassette tape for permanent enjoyment. One of these grandmothers amplified her tale with a special Swedish hymn from her childhood. She sang and played it on the piano, with descriptions of a turn-of-the-century Christmas in Minnesota and the snowy, early-morning sled trip to church, where this hymn was always sung in excited reverence as her own father played the organ.

Some families make up stories by going around in a circle and cutting off each member after three minutes. Then the next member continues until a set time when the story has to end. Such stories don't need to be silly, but they are apt to turn out that way before they are over. It is a pleasure to have these recordings of the children's voices in later years when everything has changed. We can't stop that change, and shouldn't try. But we can keep mementos so the past is never lost to us. ﹐

Another possibility is having a "radio show" like "Jac-kanory," each member reading a bit of literature that he especially likes. Family members can also interview each other, inquiring about friends, hobbies, pets, opinions, accomplishments, or frustrations, as if they were real man-on-the-street interviews. Some children—and parents—like to invent commercials to go between the interviews.

A more imaginative kind of "radio program" would be spontaneous dramatizations, setting up a situation such as a family who receives a telegram announcing that an unknown great-uncle has died and left them a million dollars. Or, for more structure, each family member can take the part of a character in a simple story they all know, such as "Goldilocks and the Three Bears," and act it out spontaneously, with or without a narrator. This can also be done with short Bible stories.

Families that enjoy this kind of thing can go on with scripts, borrowed or written at home, and sound effects and music. Some members may want to record entire hours of their favorite poetry or humor or inspirational material to listen to while they exercise or rest. Two teenage boys once developed such an elaborate adaptation of a humorous piece of literature that they took it to a conference and sold copies to interested people for the price of the tape, just for fun. Their production was almost four hours long!

We do not all have that kind of dramatic flair and dedication. But every family interchange is laden with character and meaning for the listener who has ears to hear it. Just recording some mealtime conversations and bedtime reading and talks is well worth the effort. Many of us have the magic means at our fingertips.

A word fitly spoken, Solomon said, is like apples of gold in a silver setting. There is really no shortage of those golden apples. Our world is full of words of wisdom, humor, beauty, and love if we but listen.

·American Bible Society, 1865 Broadway, New York, NY 10023.

Christian Nurture and Values

Remember these commands and cherish them. . . . Teach them to your children. Talk about them when you are at home and when you are away, when you are resting and when you are working.

Deuteronomy 11:18-19

A PROTESTANT GEOGRAPHY BOOK of 1818 included this kind of information about foreign countries:

Q. What do the I-tal-i-ans wor-ship?
A. They wor-ship i-dols and a piece of bread.
Q. Would not God be ang-ry that I-tal-i-ans wor-ship i-dols and a piece of bread?
A. God is ang-ry.

This is a vivid example of how homes and schools have often tried to impart religious values to children in the

147

heart of their general education and entertainment. That is a fine ideal. But all too often the education or entertainment has been diminished by the well-intentioned but misguided and second-rate Christian nurture.

Obviously the basic book for Christian training in the home is *The Book.* But how can the very young or older people with limited ability profit from such extremely varied and inexhaustibly rich and complex literature?

First, there are the predigested bits of Scripture that are always available for very young children. The eighty-six inexpensive Arch books, often written in rhyme, with vividly colored pictures of varying quality, are generally beloved by preschoolers. Over twenty-one million have been published so far. They are lively, brief, simple, and interesting.

There are also dozens and dozens of Bible story picture books available, some telling only one story and others telling many. *The Bible in Pictures for Little Eyes* by Kenneth Taylor contains 184 illustrated one-paragraph accounts of events in the Old and New Testaments, each with three questions. For over twenty years this has been the most popular survey of the entire Bible for children near kindergarten age. The quaint and sentimental old colored pictures delight many children who find them novel today.

Jesus, the Friend of Children is a large new picture book, illustrated by the famous team Richard and Frances Hook. It includes almost fifty brief stories of Jesus' life, each faced by a full-color picture. It is handsome and impressive.

The Living Story of Jesus, on the other hand, traces the life of Christ in almost twice as many stories and is made up almost entirely of actual passages from *The Living*

148

Bible. It is more advanced and difficult than *Jesus, the Friend of Children.*

Needless to say, countless picture books with Bible texts, often from the King James Version, come and go through the years. One of those that is very beautiful is *And It Came to Pass,* the Christmas story illustrated by Caldecott winner Leonard Weisgard.

For beginning readers there are two sets of Bible story primers, provided by Zondervan and Standard publishers. There are also plenty of children's Bibles to choose from. Some are merely adult Bibles with illustrations. Others omit the parts of the Bible that won't be meaningful to children and try to simplify the vocabulary and ideas, often adding colored illustrations. Prominent examples are Golden Press's handsome *Children's Bible,* Pearl Buck's literary *The Story Bible,* Concordia's *Holy Bible for Children,* Word's large *Children's New Testament,* and David C. Cook's two unique sets of paperback books that cover the entire Bible in skillfully composed comic strips—"The Picture Bible for All Ages" in black and white and the larger "Picture Bible in Color." Understandably, Hebrews through Revelation is covered in three pages. It is hardly comic strip material. These picture-strip Bibles are a good preview or review for all ages. Other companies have brought out separate Bible stories in actual comic books.

There are so many good Bible versions today that it is hard to go wrong. But two should not be overlooked. First is the Good News Bible: Today's English Version (1976). It is in the simplest possible standard English, full of easy introductions, outlines, definitions, maps, and other aids, as well as appropriate line illustrations.

The Good News Bible is one of the newest; the King James (or Authorized) Bible is the oldest still in use.

149

Many uninformed people have thought it was the original version of the Word of God, instead of one translation among many. Admittedly, the Authorized Version is no longer our most accurate version; there are definite minor errors in it. And it is written in the archaic English that Shakespeare used; therefore many of the correct passages are misunderstood by today's readers.

For meaning, it would be a shame to limit oneself to the Authorized Version. But for beauty it is a shame to ignore it. Its eloquence and stately cadences are almost unrivaled in English literature. Countless children have read it, scarcely knowing what it meant but captivated by the vigor, poetry, and mystery of it all. Since the Holy Book of Christianity in its 1611 version just happens to be one of the greatest works of literature of all time, Christian families might as well use this treasure occasionally and enjoy this part of our cultural heritage.

Just seventeen years after the King James Bible broke upon the world—and was rejected by some conservative Christians as too modern—a baby boy was born into a very poor family in an obscure English village. They gave him England's commonest name—John. Mr. Bunyan was a humble tinsmith, but he sent John to the free school in the village long enough for him to learn to read and write. Then he became a tinker—a mender of tin pans. John was drafted into the army as a teenager, escaped death by a hair, returned to be one of the leading village rowdies, and then married a poverty-stricken but virtuous girl when he was about twenty-one.

She had nothing but a couple of religious books that she had inherited from her father, and they read them. Soon John was studying the King James Bible, was converted, and at twenty-five he was not only a mender of tin pots, but also a lay preacher.

When he was thirty-two he was caught preaching in a farmhouse and thrown into the county jail for twelve years. There he wrote *Grace Abounding* and other works and was allowed to preach to his visitors. When he was forty-four the law was changed, allowing laymen to preach, and he returned to his wife and children. But the law was soon reversed, and he was locked up in the town jail for six months more.

It was during this time in prison that he wrote his immortal classic *Pilgrim's Progress.* In the first sentence he said he entered a den and dreamed a dream. The den was really his prison cell; the dream, the story he was inspired to write.

Bunyan waited until 1678 to publish the book, because some friends had advised against it. Beloved by both children and adults, it sold 100,000 copies in ten years while Bunyan was busy as a Baptist pastor. In 1688, when he was only sixty, he rode from Reading to London in a cold rain, took ill, and died. About one hundred and twenty years later young John Newbery took the same trip to set up his famous children's book business.

It is said that for over two centuries most homes in England had two books if no others—the King James Bible and *Pilgrim's Progress,* two of the finest works of English literature. The first was perfected by a committee of brilliant scholars; the second was composed by a poor uneducated country man in his jail cell.

Unfortunately, *Pilgrim's Progress* seems to have become a classic in Mark Twain's sense of the word—"A book which people praise and don't read." Even people who despise the Christian teaching in it readily agree that it is one of the great works of English literature. But the handsomest current edition, illustrated by Caldecott-winning artist Robert Lawson and first published by Lip-

151

pincott in 1939, turns out not to be the real *Pilgrim's Progress* at all. It is an extensive revision, produced by Mary Godolphin in 1884. This edition not only cuts the story down to 1/5 of its length—which might be all right—but rewords every sentence. She has left the language almost as old-fashioned as ever, but has changed *burden* to *load, wilderness* to *wild waste, trembled* to *shook, children* to *sweet babes*—and so on. The entire book has been changed to words of one syllable! In the first sentence alone she took out *walking, reading, lighted, certain,* and more.

Furthermore, in this 1884 edition the publisher announced proudly that he was selling *Robinson Crusoe, The Swiss Family Robinson,* and *Aesop's Fables* in the same uniform one-syllable style! Since Bunyan's flowing prose is utterly superb—except when he stops to preach a bit—all children who read this choppy version, the one most apt to be in public libraries, are getting only a staccato abbreviation of the story.

Little Pilgrim's Progress by Helen L. Taylor that sells in many Christian bookstores as an easy-to-read version is not that at all. Taylor has changed Pilgrim from the married father of four children, who repents his adult sins, to a sweet little boy whose mother is dead. She has changed Pilgrim's wife Christiana, who had four growing sons, into a sweet little orphan girl with a baby sister and two brothers to care for. All the rest of the story has to be changed accordingly.

Whatever the merits of Taylor's *Little Pilgrim's Progress,* it is no closer to the real thing than Mary Godolphin's rewriting was. Goodness knows how many people read one or the other and think they have read Bunyan's masterpiece.

Pilgrim's Progress in Today's English by James Thomas is

a simplified rendition of the story, which adds a bit here and leaves out a bit there but generally gives the reader what Bunyan intended. It serves well for people who want the message without the unique literary style. However, anyone who can do so without undue frustration would do well to read *Pilgrim's Progress* as Bunyan wrote it. As C. S. Lewis said, "We must attribute Bunyan's style to a perfect natural ear, a great sensibility for the idiom and cadence of popular speech, a long experience in addressing unlettered audiences, and a freedom from bad models." It's nice to keep in touch with roots like that.

Non-Christians claim that children enjoy the story as a literal journey and no more, missing all the Christian allegory. That seems highly questionable, since Bunyan makes his allegory so vivid and pointed. One problem for children reading *Pilgrim's Progress* could be Bunyan's conviction that only a very few Christians get to the Celestial City and that the danger of falling into hell stretches clear up to the gate of heaven. There is a strong element of narrowness and terror in the book along with its heroism, humor, and pleasures.

Parents who feel that the life view is a bit too negative can explain to their children that Bunyan was severely persecuted for his religion and that in his day sincere believers tended to be more intolerant of other believers.

We may not agree with Bunyan that a Christian is very apt to fall from the grace of God, but we can all identify with many of Pilgrim's follies and triumphs and learn along with him and Christiana. One verse seems worth memorizing:

He that is down need fear no fall,
He that is low no pride,
He that is humble ever shall
Have God to be his guide.

153

C. S. Lewis gave a talk on BBC radio near the end of his life paying tribute to *Pilgrim's Progress.* He ended with the sentence, "But most, I fancy, have discovered that to be born is to be exposed to delights and miseries greater than imagination could have anticipated; that the choice of ways at any cross-road may be more important than we think; and that short cuts may lead to very nasty places."

Today someone could end a talk about Lewis's own *Chronicles of Narnia* with the very same sentence. Like *Pilgrim's Progress,* these stories warn about short cuts, stress the importance of choices, and portray the delights and miseries of life with extreme clarity.

The Narnian Chronicles have already been described in the chapter on contemporary fantasy, but they are more than fantasy. They are Christian fantasy. They are not real allegory, like *Pilgrim's Progress,* but they teach Christian truth just as strongly in their own way. Much children's literature is highly moral, inspiring, and uplifting; but the stories of Narnia are also imbued with Christian theology. It would be hard to think of a more successful blending of entertainment with Christian teaching.

Lewis would be unhappy if parents ever spoiled the stories for children by turning them into Bible lessons. He meant for Narnia to work its own work in the readers' imaginations. He would probably not object, however, to the kit *Voyage to Narnia: C. S. Lewis and the Christian Faith,* published by David C. Cook, full of questions, ideas, audiovisual aids, and other helps to an abundant enjoyment of all seven books. It is designed for use in young adult groups but could be used in families—or even by individuals.

Cook also offers a packet really intended for use in schools that could be used at home. It is called "Learning about Values: Teaching Pictures" for elementary school children. It includes sixteen colored posters and a booklet for teaching sixteen key values, such as honesty and humor. Each value is demonstrated in an entertaining sample reading from a selected book for children, followed by descriptions of a few other good children's books that demonstrate the same value. This could be an excellent way to interest the family in value discussions and good reading.

Another very unusual set is offered by Concordia and available through Christian bookstores. It is called "The Purple Puzzle Tree," a set of six record albums telling the story of Tickle the Tiger with sound effects and music. Each record has six colorful story booklets so children can follow along as the record plays. The books can be used without the record albums, but the art work is inferior to the especially fine music and sound.

The first four albums are a fanciful but scrupulously correct retelling of the high points of the Old Testament. The last two albums do the same for the New Testament. God's creative, sustaining, and redemptive love for man as expressed throughout the Bible is summarized brilliantly in this imaginative set of records and books. They present an in-depth understanding of Bible themes that few adult church members have; yet they are enjoyed by kindergartners. Except for families that dislike unusual or "frivolous" approaches to traditional topics, this is an extremely meaningful overview of the Bible, and it can't be matched. It is good for people of any age, so long as they can tolerate a little good-natured silliness along with their theology. It makes very happy material for family devotions.

The book *Happiness Is Family Time Together* (1975) by Lois Bock and Miji Working is not really children's litera-

155

ture. It is an unusual departure from the ordinary idea of family devotions. The authors suggest many constructive substitutes for "reading at" children.

For families who like traditional devotional materials, the most enduringly popular books are probably *Little Visits with God* and *More Little Visits with God* by Jahamann and Simon. There are many similar books with simple anecdotes illustrating moral or theological points. Some children enjoy these, and others find them too pious or boring.

One of the loveliest of the countless prayer books for children is *Moments with God,* published by Regina.

The Mustard Seed Library published by Creation House is unusual in that it presents the charismatic experience of Christianity directly to small children.

Agnes Sanford wrote a pair of unusual but enduring books for children, *Let's Believe* and *A Pasture for Peterkin.* Their clear teaching about how inner thought and prayer life effects outer circumstances is bold indeed. The rather sweet old-fashioned approach is balanced with strong faith and briskly practical psychology so the two books speak to parents as well as children.

Bettie Wilson Story's *Summer of Jubilee* (1977) is an example of the modern problem story in a Christian context. Fourteen-year-old Marte has as problems: an artificial leg, sudden dislocation from her beloved lifetime home to a new community, an unwelcome and permanent roommate—her beautiful and arrogant cousin, fear of water because of the accident that cost her her leg, and the unexpected unemployment of her father. The story includes some do-it-yourself Gestalt psychology, interesting information about marine biology, and wise, wonderful parents reminiscent of Madeleine L'Engle's *Meet the Austins.* Characters are free from stereotyped sex roles, and Christianity is woven in unobtrusively as the family orientation.

Children have long enjoyed *Peter Piper, Missionary Parakeet* by Gertrude Warner, which describes the amusing true adventures of an unusual bird. Now children can read the evocative little fantasy *Semo: A Dolphin's Search for Christ* (1977) by S. G. Harrell. Semo was a dolphin who lived at the time of Christ, and he played a loving part in the lives of both Peter and Christ. But the most moving Christian animal story of all—one that can bring tears to the eyes of almost anyone—is the story "Robin Redbreast" by Selma Lagerlof.

Scott O'Dell, winner of both the Newbery Award and the Hans Christian Andersen Award, ardently admires William Tyndale for sacrificing his life to give England the Bible in English. Tyndale's translation, for which he died at the stake in 1536, is the basis of our King James Version. In 1975 O'Dell published *The Hawk That Dare Not Hunt by Day,* a novel based upon Tyndale's life. O'Dell did research for two years, visiting England and the continent more than once in preparation for this story, which is rich in historical details about smuggling, sea life, and the Black Death. It is a superb contribution to the rather scanty supply of literature for children about our Christian heritage.

Other individual Christian books of special interest include:

The Bronze Bow by Elizabeth Speare
God's Troubadour by Sophie Jewett (illustrations by Giotto)
John Wesley by May McNeer (illustrated by her husband Lynd Ward)
The Mighty Ones: Great Men and Women of Early Bible Days by Meindert De Jong

HOW TO GROW A YOUNG READER

Songs of the Sun by Francis of Assisi (illustrated by Elizabeth Orton Jones)

Of course children move into adult Christian literature as soon as they are ready. Much standard Christian fare such as Catherine Marshall's *Christy* is easily read by mature twelve year olds. There is a phenomenal abundance of adult Christian literature today and not nearly so much that is specifically Christian for children.

However, there are dozens of adventure tales, animal parables, family stories, missionary stories, and tales set out in the country or back in the past that are printed in inexpensive editions; these range from the good quality of Patricia St. John's stories to humble but happy Archie comic books. It seems to be extremely difficult for highly competent writers to produce distinctly Christian fiction of great merit. The more doctrine the book includes, the lower it usually ranks as literature. The finer the writing, the less specific doctrine one is apt to find. C. S. Lewis, the master in this field, urged authors not to force specific morals and doctrine into their fiction. It won't ring true, he advised, unless it is inevitable.

Popular series of Christian adventure books continue to entertain and try to inspire young readers: the old Paul Hutchens's *Sugar Creek Gang,* the new Mary Christian *Goosehill Gang,* Paul White's worthy *Jungle Doctor* books, and the *Danny Orlis* series by Bernard Palmer.

The Austin Boys Adrift by Ken Anderson was a Christmas present to one of your authors in 1944. The pages are brittle, musty, and browning, but the print is still clear. At the end the two too-perfect Austin boys have suddenly become international heroes and have also led tough anti-religious Lieutenant Wilson to the Lord. Tim has miraculously survived a burst appendix, followed by a successful enemy aircraft attack, a crash at sea, several days on a raft without food and water, a violent storm, and belated surgery. Jim speaks to Tim at the end of the story:

> 'You know, the Lord really does things for a fellow. I wish every fellow in the world had Him for a friend. . . . It makes life lots more fun, doesn't it, Tim?'

> 'It sure does, Jim.'

> Then, looking silently at each other for a moment as they gripped each other's hands, Jim and Tim Austin said that as long as they lived they were going to seek God's will in everything, for they had learned beyond a doubt that God leads those who put their trust in Him.

Actually, this is poor prose. But at least one boy who received it for Christmas came to love great literature anyway—and to believe the basic message that the Austin boys share with Bunyan's Pilgrim: "God leads those who put their trust in Him."

There is a store sticker at the front of that book. It says "Christian Reading in Christian Homes." It's an old ideal and a good one.

12

Roots and Fruits

The Literature of Our Lives

'There was once a little princess who—'
'But, Mr. Author, why do you always write about princesses?'
'Because every little girl is a princess.'
'You will make them vain if you tell them that.'
'Not if they understand what I mean.'
'Then what do you mean?'
'What do you mean by a princess?'
'The daughter of a king.'
'Very well, then every little girl is a princess. . . .'

George MacDonald
The Princess and the Goblin

"WE'RE LOOKING FOR PEOPLE to write children's books," the ad says. "We need writers. There are over 150 publishers of books for children and more than 250 magazines, all of which have a need for writers. . . . Have you ever read a children's story and said 'I can do better

160

than that'? Have you ever deplored the lack of good new literature for young readers? . . . The market is enormous. Editors and publishers of children's literature are searching for talented writers. . . . Last year, more than 30 million children's books were published, producing total sales of over 170 million dollars! . . ."

But the enthusiastic company that is urging people to become writers for children is only a correspondence school. It wants to teach basic writing techniques to would-be writers for a price. It may offer very good instruction. But there is no shortage of writers for children.

Quite the contrary, editors and publishers are already besieged with truckloads of manuscripts they can't use. Many publishers return about a hundred manuscripts a week. They hardly ever accept one that comes in uninvited.

There are untold thousands of Americans who have written stories for children that will never be printed. There are enough unpublished books to fill a large—but rather dull—library.

Editors really are always on the lookout for phenomenally good writers—or writers whose sales might be phenomenal. But they groan as they plow through the ordinary material that pours in all year long. One editor claimed that she received several amateurishly written stories about twins every month. Blond twins. So a writer friend teased her by mailing in the following beginning and asking for a large advance payment.

At the Seashore

Billy and Betty Williams had been twins all their lives. They both had sparkling blue eyes and curly blond hair, and they were both nine years old. They lived in a white house in

161

the country with their father, Mr. Williams, and their mother, Mrs. Williams, and their dog Spot.

One morning Mrs. Williams said, "I have a surprise for you. We are going to have a vacation at the seashore. Pack your suitcases now, and we will leave after lunch when dad returns from the city."

Everyone was happy—even Spot.

That book has not yet been continued.

Aspiring writers should always take heart, however, when they remember that both Dr. Seuss and Richard Adams had their first books—which were far from trite—rejected by many, many publishers before they were accepted and became immensely popular. Editors do guess wrong about some children's books.

Very few writers of children's literature who get published can support themselves with their craft. Many of the best had the privilege of an expensive university education, many have been aided by financial support from spouses or inheritance, and most have to write after regular work hours—which leaves little time for anything else. For parents, especially, that isn't easy.

But every parent can become a successful author at home. Many mothers start to fill in a baby book for their first child but bog down as the months and years fly by. Alas, when did baby cut his molars, and what was baby's second present from Santa, and when did baby first go to the barber shop? The book is apt to go totally blank long before its subject gets to the university degrees, civic honors, and military exploits section sometimes found at the end.

Nevertheless, a baby book can be a good help at first, especially if the parent adds locks of hair and funny stories about baby and relatives, covering over boring pages with things that are more interesting like pictures and special greeting cards or little smudges of the strained beets that baby threw on the wall. Later that young person will marvel at these proofs that he was ever such a funny little animal and so loved. One family even taped in the sliver of pink soap with four small clear tooth marks, a memento of the day their toddler checked to see if pink soap tastes like candy.

Silly as all that sounds, it is a rare child who does not take special pleasure in looking at "*my* baby book" later. It makes a child feel special.

What children seem to enjoy most is a simple collection of many of the funny or quaint things that they said in their early years. They still enjoy these collections when they are adults. Because such a collection will probably range from age one to about eight, the parent is wise to begin with a loose-leaf notebook that includes a pocket where scraps of paper can be tucked temporarily.

If parents usually carry paper and pen when going out, as many do, and if there are plenty of pens and pads around the house, they can often scribble down amusing sayings at the time, with the date if possible. These can be tucked into the notebook pocket later and eventually copied onto the pages—typed there by parents who are fortunate enough to know how. The first sayings can be mere baby talk, and the later ones will include all kinds of linguistic and psychological subtleties.

Here are just a few from two very ordinary little boys:

"The Lord is my shepherd, I shall not want him."
"I brush my teeth so I won't get academies."
"Dad, if Hawaii is part of the United States, how did it get so far
   away?"
"After infinity comes trinity."

"Dad, your hair has a hole in the middle."
"I don't want *this* piece of bread. This piece is the knee."

Drawings, notes, and letters by the children provide samples of their growth and personality well worth saving. They can be stashed in a special drawer or, if time allows, arranged in a scrapbook. One grandmother even offered to take all these pictures and memorabilia and combine them into a "This Is Your Life" book for her grandchildren. The pictures were used to illustrate the story-commentary she wrote.

Descriptions of family trips and special times or celebrations can also be a pleasure to read later, especially if feelings are emphasized instead of lists of details.

And photo albums, of course, the picture books of family life, never lose their interest. Sets of slides and home movies capture even more of life, but they are less apt to be used for browsing.

Some children take an interest in writing diaries. This gives a little sustained writing practice, which is worthwhile. Besides that, it helps children become more aware of how a year passes and how they spend their time, money, and energy. They like to put a part of their lives into book form, wondering what will happen on all the blank pages to come. These diaries should be secret, if they are to be at all exciting.

One of the most moving books of our century happens to be a child's diary. It is the story of Anne Frank, a Jewish girl in Holland who was hiding from the Nazis with her family. The Nazis destroyed Anne Frank; but they did not find her diary. It is ours to read today with smiles and tears.

Journals are generally much more creative and enriching than diaries. They, too, are usually private; but there could be a family journal for members who are close and supportive. A large loose-leaf notebook would allow members to draw, write, or type on their own sheets of three-hole paper, then date and include them, day by day or week by week. All members could examine and think about the contributions of the other members. Everyone could put in his or her fears, hopes, joys, interests, responses, discoveries, ideas, poems, stories, dreams, songs, prayers, and letters to oneself or to the rest of the family.

Just as an in-depth private journal can put an individual more in touch with his inner self and his capacities, so a family journal might put a family more in touch with itself. The story it gradually told would be the inner story of a group of unique, growing people. Just making this book together could influence that story.

Here the humblest contribution is as valuable as the most artistic. A truly skillful sonnet by one member is no "better" than an awkward bit of verse with misspelled words.

One September an English teacher asked her young teenage students to write on the old topic "What I Did Last Summer." (She believed it was a good old topic.) A girl named Janet told about being the only survivor of an August traffic accident that killed her father and brother. She said she would not have shared her sorrow if she had not been asked to write that paper, and that writing about it helped. She ended by deciding that the summer of her childhood was suddenly over.

Each one of us will someday reflect upon how we spent the summer of our lives. There is no more fascinating and profound story. It began "Once upon a time," and it will eventually end beyond all imagining.

FURTHER RECOMMENDED READING FOR PARENTS

Egoff, Sheila, G. T. Stubbs, and L. F. Ashley, eds. *Only Connect: Readings on Children's Literature.* Oxford: Oxford University Press, 1969.

Newbery Medal Books, 1929-1955 with Acceptance Papers, Biographies of Award Winners, and an Appraisal of the Winning Books by Elizabeth Nesbit.

Newbery and Caldecott Medal Books 1956-1965 with Acceptance Papers, Biographies of the Award Winners and Evaluating Articles by Elizabeth H. Gross, Carolyn Horovitz, and Norma R. Fryatt.

Newbery and Caldecott Medal Books 1966-1975 with Acceptance Papers by the Award Winners, Biographical Notes, and Evaluating Essays by John Rowe Townsend, Barbara Bader, and Elizabeth Johnson.

Townsend, John Rowe. *Written for Children,* rev. ed. Philadelphia: Lippincott, 1974.

Walsh, Frances, *That Eager Zest.* Philadelphia: Lippincott, 1961.

Wintle, Justin, and Emma Fisher. *The Pied Pipers: Interviews with Influential Creators of Children's Literature.* New York: Paddington Press, 1974. (Twenty-two interviews, two letters.)